Writing POEMS

Michael Harrison and Christopher Stuart-Clark

Oxford University Press

Oxford University Press, Walton Street, Oxford OX2 6DP

Oxford New York Toronto
Delhi Bombay Calcutta Madras Karachi
Kuala Lumpur Singapore Hong Kong Tokyo
Nairobi Dar es Salaam Cape Town
Melbourne Auckland Madrid

and associated companies in
Berlin Ibadan

Oxford is trade mark of Oxford University Press
© Selection and notes 1985
Michael Harrison and Christopher Stuart-Clark

First published 1985
Reprinted 1986, 1987, 1988, 1990, 1991, 1994

ISBN 0 19 834270 5

The publishers would like to thank the following for their
permission to reproduce photographs:

Barnaby's Picture Library pp. 52, 53; Janet and Colin Bord
pp. 28, 29; Allan Burgis p. 123; J Allan Cash Photo Library
pp. 72, 73; John Cleare/Mountain Camera p. 63; Bruce
Coleman p. 50; Daily Telegraph Colour Library pp. 67, 103;
Richard and Sally Greenhill pp. 41, 64–65; John Jennings
p. 49; Rob Judges p. 44; John Twinning pp. 6, 7, 9, 10, 12.

Illustrations are by Cecilia Eales, Gecko Ltd., Sue Heap,
Terry Kennett, Robert Kettell, and Nick Sharratt.

Cover illustration by Nick Sharratt.

Typeset in Lintron 202 by
Graphicraft Typesetters Limited, Hong Kong
Printed in Hong Kong

Contents

For the teacher

There are two ways into writing poetry:

1. Through content: We need to write poems about something. Good poetry needs the commitment of the writer. Ted Hughes' *Poetry in the Making* is the most stimulating book to take this way in. We can use our experience through:

Looking: the close, brooding attention we need to draw well is also necessary to write well.

Thinking: looking honestly into oneself.

In practice these two approaches are intertwined.

2. Through form: Poems fit words into a pattern. Children tend to write either free verse or rhyming doggerel. We believe that children's poetry should have some structure. Such simple techniques as word-shapes, haiku, acrostics, 'snapshots' provide manageable forms so that children can experience that excitement and satisfaction of success in fitting form and content together. The first part of this book stresses form; the second, content – but all the poems are examples of both.

The place of criticism

We should all the time be trying to build up our pupils' honest confidence in their own judgement. Criticism of anything children have put their hearts into must be sensitive and tentative, but we do them no service if we accept everything equally. Group discussion of each other's writing is very helpful, especially in the early stages. Criticism at the final draft stage is too late to be anything except harmful.

With experience we can encourage out pupils to use the four ways into a poem we use in the companion anthologies, *Poems 1* and *Poems 2:*

Story

What is my poem about?
Is it clear?
Have I said what I want to say about it?

Feeling

What feelings am I trying to provoke in the reader?
Have I been honest in my writing?

Pattern

Have I chosen the best pattern for what I want to say?
Have I managed to fit the words to the pattern?
Have I written nonsense, or tortured the words to make them fit?

Image

Have I written in words that create pictures?
Have I used my senses?
Do my images clash?
Are they stale or predictable?

A lesson pattern

1. **Stimulus:**
    Reading a poem or poems
    Looking at something
    Discussion
    Thinking

2. **First draft:**
    It is important that we don't accept that poems normally
    appear in finished form.
    At this stage jot down any ideas
                              words
                              phrases.
    You can collect the ideas on the board, or work in groups.

3. **Pattern making:**
    Try to fit the words to the pattern you have chosen.

4. **Criticism:**
    It can help to come back to the poem next day.
    Three basic questions:
    Have I used the best words?
    Have I been honest?
    Does the pattern fit?

5. **Revision:**
    This is perhaps the most difficult, and most important, stage.

6. **And final draft for publication:**
    Read it out to the class.
    Pin it on the wall.
    Photocopy it for class broadsheet.
    Add to pupil's own poetry file.

In the work pages to each section this sign ▶ introduces ideas which the teacher will need to plan.

Snapshots

Snow and Ice Poems

Our street is dead lazy
especially in winter.
Some mornings you wake up
and it's still lying there
saying nothing. Huddled
under its white counterpane.

Winter
morning.
Snowflakes
for breakfast.
The street
outside
quiet
as a
long
white
bandage.

Roger McGough

Shadows

Chunks of night
Melt
In the morning sun.
One lonely one
Grows legs
And follows me
To school.

Patricia Hubbell

The Tree-creeper

I saw a little mouse
Run up a tree – then twitch
Out pointed delicate wings,
And flitter away on the breeze.

John Heath Stubbs

Autumn in Regent's Park

Under a tree
St Francis
in an old mac
preaches sermons
to the birds
from a crumpled brown
paper bag.

Gerda Mayer

In the Stable: Christmas Haiku

Donkey

My long ears can hear
Angels singing, but my song
Would wake the baby.

Ox

I stand patiently.
It is busy here tonight.
Who is this baby?

Sheep

On bleak hills my wool
Keeps me warm. Is your baby
Snug enough in straw?

Camel

I have brought treasure
But kneel now to the maker
Of sun, moon, and stars.

Dog

I will not bark but
Lie, head on paws, eyes watching
All these visitors.

Cat

I wash my feet. For
This baby all should be clean.
My purr will soothe him.

Owl

My round eyes look down.
No starlit hunting this night:
Peace to little ones!

Mouse

In this place I feel
Safe. This baby will not scream
If he sees quiet me.

Spider

My fine web sparkles:
Indoor star in the roof's night
Over the baby.

Dove

I decorate this
Manger with an olive branch.
It promises peace.

John Corben

Animals

The ANT's a marching shopping-list,
An exclamation mark on legs:
She balances a hundred eggs
And looks a mile for one she's missed.

There on the carpet! The wet RAT poured
Into its body's pulsing sack,
Tied with a whisker. Its raw tail
Defends its presence like a sword.

The TIGER flares in total darkness,
Sergeant-striped with traffic eyes,
And in this technicolor nightmare
Glows in continual surprise.

The WHALE yawns like a handbag, scores
Of boats are bobbing, harpoons raised:
The moment's endless, mesmerised
By the dress-circle of his jaws.

John Fuller

A Farm Picture

Through the ample open door of the peaceful country barn,
A sunlit pasture field with cattle and horses feeding,
And haze and vista, and the far horizon fading away.

Walt Whitman

Poplar

Propped up
against the pale
wall of the sky,
small birds
snipped from
black paper
pose there
in silhouette:
Summer's dark plume is
Winter's besom broom.

Gerda Mayer

Wind and Silver

Greatly shining,
The Autumn moon floats in the sky;
And the fish ponds shake their backs and flash their dragon scales
As she passes over them.

Amy Lowell

The Torch

On my northwestern coast in the midst of the night a fisherman's
   group stands watching,
Out on the lake that expands before them, others are spearing
   salmon,
The canoe, a dim shadowy thing, moves across the black water,
Bearing a torch ablaze at the prow.

Walt Whitman

Autumn

A touch of cold in the Autumn night –
I walked abroad,
And saw the ruddy moon lean over a hedge
Like a red-faced farmer.
I did not stop to speak, but nodded,
And round about were the wistful stars
With white faces like town children.

T. E. Hulme

Above the Dock

Above the quiet dock in midnight,
Tangled in the tall mast's corded height,
Hangs the moon. What seemed so far away
Is but a child's balloon, forgotten after play.

T. E. Hulme

Willow

A willow kneels by the riverbank
And throws her hair out over the clear water.
Her light loose tresses, brushed by wind,
Trail in the stream's current.
Small leaves join the water-boatmen
And drift on the drifting water.
One tree kneels by the bank, one in the river:
Both are beautiful, both forever in movement.

Clive Sansom

Snapshots

Words can make pictures in your mind.
We can think of a poem as a **snapshot** – a piece of time frozen for ever.
A snapshot can freeze people, places, events, feelings, ideas.

Snapshots are often written as **haiku**.
A **haiku** is a three line poem in which you have to count the syllables.

5 in the first line	Moon's Day: the first day
7 in the second	Ought to shine in the week like
5 in the third	New minted silver.
17 altogether.	

January to December (page 29) is a haiku poem.
In the Stable (page 9) is a series of haiku snapshots.

Snapshots should usually be short, just a few lines.
To write a good snapshot you should –
Look carefully and choose what is the most important thing. This is like looking through a camera's viewfinder. Put a frame round the scene in your mind. Do you want to 'zoom' in?
Choose the important details, the ones that will create a picture
Choose the best words.

1 Start with the classroom. When you close your eyes, what do you remember most clearly? Use that as the centre of your **snapshot**. Write a four line poem.

2 Try to turn some of your snapshots into **haiku**. Try to get one clear picture in each haiku.

3 You can write **snapshots** about imaginary monsters and imaginary places.

4 Write **snapshots** like riddles. Describe something in one clear picture without saying what it is.

▶ Writers can go for a walk with their notebooks and take **snapshots**: around the school, streets, machines, people, weather, by night and by day. You can collect together the snapshots from the class and mount them to look like photographs in an album.
Use the snapshot riddles as a guessing game or mount them with a picture clue to the answer.

one

t
hi
s
snowflake
(a
  li
    ght
  in
g)
is upon a gra
v
es
t
one

e. e. cummings

Snake

Snake glides
   through grass
      over
         pebbles
            forked tongue
         working
      never
speaking
      but its
         body
            whispers
               listen

Keith Bosley

Development

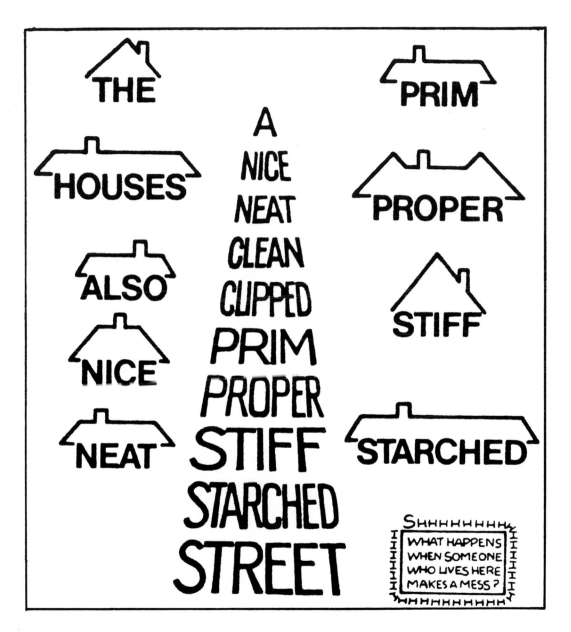

Robert Froman

Ping-Pong

Swatted between bats
The celluloid ball
Leaps on unseen elastic
Skimming the taut net

Sliced   Spun
Screwed   Cut
Dabbed   Smashed

Ping   Point   Pong
Pong   Service   Ping
Bing   Bong
Bong   Bing

Ding   Point   Dong
Dong   Service   Ding
Ting   Tong
Tang   Tong

Angled   Point   Slipped
Cut   Service   Driven
Floated   Carressed
Driven   THWACKED   Hammered
                  Point

Bit		Bat
Tip		Tap
Slip		Slap
Zip		Zap
Whip		Whap
	Point	
	Service	
Left		Yes
Right		Yes
Twist		Yes
Skids		Yes
Eighteen		Seventeen
Eighteen		All
Nineteen		Eighteen
Nineteen		All
Twenty		Nineteen
	Point	
	Service	
Forehand		Backhand
Swerves		Yes
Rockets		Yes
Battered		Ah
Cracked		Ah

SMASHED

SMASHED

SMASHED

Gareth Owen

A fussing wind
worries the leaves
subduing
their chatter

They risk
pale undersides
exposing them
tender
to the sun

Boughs
lift
  sway
    bend
    ease
    rock
bear

Ivy
  twists
    holds
    caresses
clasps
  keeps
    garrottes
  with its seductive rope
as surely as a noose

Green rests gently
in the skirts
of larch
gleams
on polished holly leaves
spiked
with wicked barbs

Leaf
  twig
    branch
      bough
      trunk
      roots

Trunks
like beefy legs
stand easy
in the wood
toes festooned
by a scribble
of stinging nettles

Doves play
ring-o-
    ring-o
        roses
in the sunlit aisle
between the trees

Brambles
eat greedily
cruelly
into the space
beneath the trees

The umbrella spokes
of cow parsley
crackle
in a dry rehearsal
for autumn

Daisies
like
slender-fingered
hands
offer up
their
yellow
pollen

Soft nettle green
tempts
in an unkindness
of ragged weeds

Moira Andrew

Pantomime Poem

'HE'S BEHIND YER!'
chorused the children
but the warning came too late.

The monster leaped forward
and fastening its teeth into his neck,
tore off the head.

The body fell to the floor.
'MORE' cried the children
'MORE, MORE, MORE

MORE
MORE
M(

Roger McGough

Shape poems

Keith Bosley took some ideas about a snake (page 14):

    Snake glides through grass over pebbles   forked tongue working never speaking but its body whispers   listen

and uses a snake shape   to make:

                              Snake glides
                           through grass
                        over
                              pebbles
                                   forked tongue
                     working
                  never
              speaking
                  but its
                  body
                      whispers
                    listen

1   Look at these shapes: write some ideas about the object that each represents and build them into a **shape poem**.

2   Draw your own outline shape of:
        a bicycle   a train   a supermarket shelf   a telegraph pole
        a cat   a crab   a spider   a butterfly
        and then fit ideas about each of them into a **shape.**

3   *Pantomime Poem* (page 19) uses big letters to make words seem 'louder'. Try making some ideas look like:
        sounds becoming quieter   sounds echoing   stereo-sound
        a waterfall   a train getting closer, passing and going away

4 *Ping-Pong* (page 16–17) makes your eyes follow the words as if you were actually watching some ping-pong. Look at these **patterns** of:

swimming lengths of a pool   skating on a rink

Then set out some ideas, words and sounds, in the patterns that represent the actions.
Try the same with:
    boxing in a ring   running round a track   playing hop-scotch

5 Moira Andrew (page 18) sets her ideas out at different parts of a tree, describing the trunk, branches, ground etc. Draw a cross-section of your house like this:

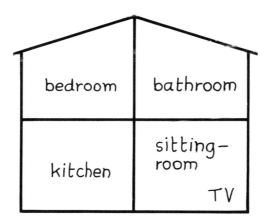

Then put in thoughts and ideas into the relevant areas.
Try this also with:
    the school-playground   a supermarket

Sequences

Proverbial Alphabet

Acorns were good
till bread was found.

Better a snotty child
than his nose wiped off.

Children are certain cares
but uncertain comforts.

Dogs bark
as they are bred.

Empty hands
no hawks allure.

Friends tie their purse
with a cobweb thread.

Gifts
blind the eyes.

Honey is sweet
but the bee stings.

Idle folk
lack no excuses.

Justice pleases few
in their own house.

Knowledge
is no burden.

Lies
have short legs.

 **M**any would be cowards
if they had courage enough.

 To burn one's house
to get rid of the mice.

 Necessity
has no holiday.

 Use
makes mastery.

 Old foxes
need no tutors.

 Vows made in storms
are forgotten in calms.

 Pigs fly in the air
with their tails forward.

 Wealth
makes wit waver.

 Quarrelling dogs
come halting home.

 eXperience is the common
schoolhouse of fools.

 Revenge is a dish
that should be eaten cold.

 **Y**ou will not believe he's bald
until you see his brains.

 Short folk
are soon angry.

 Zeal, when it is a virtue,
is a dangerous one.
Michael Richards

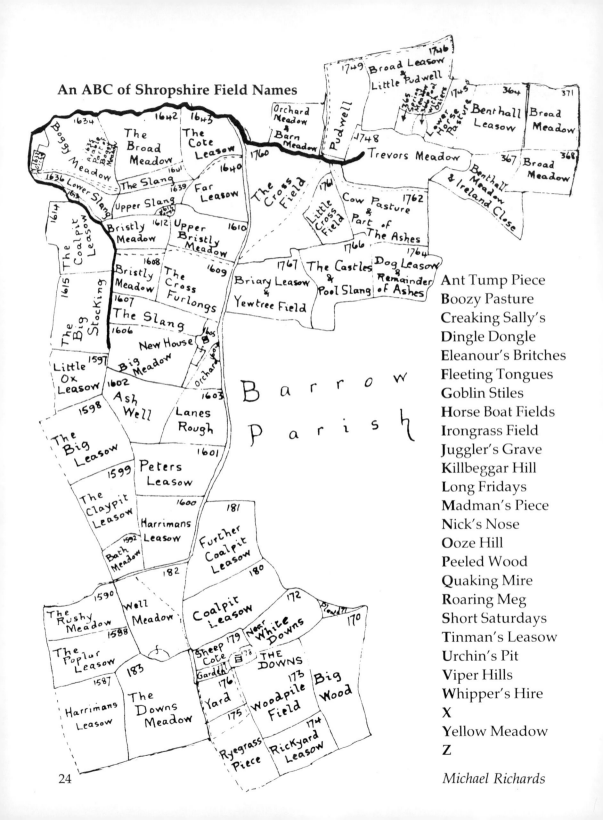

An ABC of Shropshire Field Names

Ant Tump Piece
Boozy Pasture
Creaking Sally's
Dingle Dongle
Eleanour's Britches
Fleeting Tongues
Goblin Stiles
Horse Boat Fields
Irongrass Field
Juggler's Grave
Killbeggar Hill
Long Fridays
Madman's Piece
Nick's Nose
Ooze Hill
Peeled Wood
Quaking Mire
Roaring Meg
Short Saturdays
Tinman's Leasow
Urchin's Pit
Viper Hills
Whipper's Hire
X
Yellow Meadow
Z

Michael Richards

Week of Winter Weather

On Monday icy rain poured down
and flooded drains all over town.

Tuesday's gales rent elm and ash;
dead branches came down with a crash.

On Wednesday bursts of hail and sleet:
no-one walked along our street.

Thursday stood out clear and calm:
but the sun was paler than my arm.

Friday's frost that bit your ears
was cold enough to freeze your tears.

Saturday's sky was ghostly grey;
we smashed ice on the lake today.

Christmas Eve was Sunday and
snow fell like foam across the land.

Wes Magee

Sunday smells of bacon, eggs

Sunday smells of bacon, eggs
And hot, baked, lazing cars.
Monday smells of washing
And fresh air.
Tuesday smells of less activity,
Of ironing, tea and biscuits.
Wednesday smells lonely, bleak,
Stuck there – mid of the week –
Supported by a rhyme.
Thursday is sturdier,
Smells of rich beef stew
With dumplings, we hope.
Friday smells of week-old bed-clothes
Weaving me into the body of the bed
In drowsing, rotting doze;
Yes, Friday smellz!
Splendid Saturday
Smells of shortbread, fairy-cakes,
Sausages and onions,
Apple-crumble and not-school custard.
Sunday again –
And Sunday *ought* to smell of church,
Dead mice and incense.
Sorry, but no.
It smells of ragged curtains
For home-made camps
And battered old bikes,
And friends.

Jill Campbell

Round the Town

Round the town with Billy,
Round the town with Sue,
From Sunday morning to Saturday night
With nothing else to do.

What do you do on Monday?
We look up at the sky
Waiting for a drying wind
To make the washing fly.

What do you do on Tuesday?
From underneath the stair
We see them take the wooden horse
To let the linen air.

What do you do on Wednesday?
We watch the butchers' men
Drive the frightened animals
In and out the pen.

What do you do on Thursday?
On early-closing day
We see the shops are safely locked
And the money put away.

What do you do on Friday?
The local paper's read
To find if we are still alive
Or whether we are dead.

What do you do on Saturday?
We sit and hold our breath
And see the silver cowboys
Shoot themselves to death.

What do you do on Sunday?
We listen for the bell
And pray to Christ our Saviour
To guard and keep us well.

What do you do on Monday?
We look out through the pane
And if it's wet or if it's fine
Begin all over again.

Charles Causley

27

The Garden Year

January brings the snow,
Makes our feet and fingers glow.

February brings the rain,
Thaws the frozen lake again.

March brings breezes, loud and shrill,
To stir the dancing daffodil.

April brings the primrose sweet,
Scatters daisies at our feet.

May brings flocks of pretty lambs
Skipping by their fleecy dams.

June brings tulips, lilies, roses,
Fills the children's hands with posies.

Hot July brings cooling showers,
Apricots and gillyflowers.

August brings the sheaves of corn,
Then the harvest home is borne.

Warm September brings the fruit;
Sportsmen then begin to shoot.

Fresh October brings the pheasant;
Then to gather nuts is pleasant.

Dull November brings the blast;
Then the leaves are whirling fast.

Chill December brings the sleet,
Blazing fire, and Christmas treat.

Sara Coleridge

January to December

The warm cows have gone
From the fields where grass stands up
Dead-alive like steel.

Unexpected sun
Probes the house as if someone
Had left the lights on.

Novel no longer
Snowdrops melt in the hedge, drain
Away into spring.

The heron shining
Works his way up the bright air
Above the river.

Earth dries. The sow basks
Flat out with her blue-black young,
Ears over their eyes.

The early lambs, still
Fleecy, look bulkier now
Than their shorn mothers.

In this valley full
Of bird song, the gap closes
Behind the cuckoo.

Fields of barley glimpsed
Through trees shine out like golden
Windows in winter.

Though nothing has changed –
The sun is even hotter –
Death is in the air.

Long shadows herald
Or dog every walker
In the cut-back lanes.

A crop of mist grows
Softly in the valley, lolls
Over the strawstacks.

Meadows filmed across
With rain stare up at winter
Hardening in the hills.

Patricia Beer

29

Noises from the School

Half-past-nine and the town school
Is packed and quiet. From the room in which I write
I cannot see it. I go on working and wait
For some stirring of the pool.

Somewhere it must be harvest time.
Flickering voices half an hour ago,
And a firm piano told the neighbours, 'We plough
The fields and scatter'. An odd claim

Coming from concrete and foul air
Where mortar-mixers arrive and a crane builds.
God apparently goes on living in fields
And all the singers live here.

Eleven o'clock, and the first howl
Of playtime, singular as the opening twitter
Of a dawn chorus, and soon after that the skitter
Over the yard of the first football.

Twelve o'clock. Until half-past-one
Screaming again and a harsh clattering yell:
Some child is imitating – a guinea fowl?
Of course not, a machine gun.

Quarter-to-four. The bell to go home.
Down the alley the children die away. I write
In town silence and think of the habitat
From where my comparisons come.

Patricia Beer

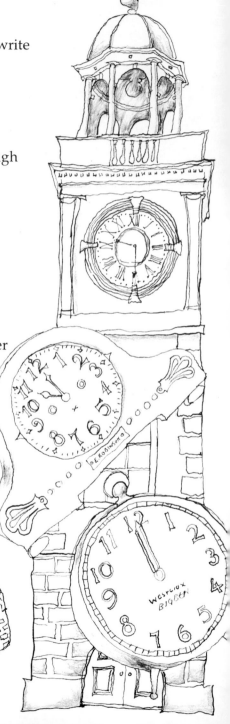

Sequences

An ABC of Shropshire Field Names (page 24) and the *Proverbial Alphabet* (page 22) are both **found poems**. They are 'found' because the writer didn't make up any of the words. He found them in a book of field names and in a book of proverbs, and carefully chose which ones to use. There are 246 field-names in Shropshire beginning with B. He chose 'Boozy Pasture' because it gives a picture of the farm workers lying in the sun during the hay harvest swigging away at their cider jars.

Both these found poems use the **sequence** of the alphabet to give a pattern. Other poems in this section have used other sequences to give pattern to the words:

    the days of the week
    the months of the year
    the divisions of the day

1   Collect your own **found poem** ABC. Try local street names, shop names, names from 'Yellow Pages', nicknames. See if you can find any specialist dictionaries.
    Choose words or phrases that create a picture in your mind.

2   Days of the week:
    Start with **wordplay**.   Monday is Moanday
                    Tuesday is . . .
    Think of an **image** for each day.
                  Monday is a big black cloud.
                  Tuesday is . . .
    Think of **colours** or **shapes** for the days.

3   You can use months and seasons in the same way.
    The **sequence** gives you a pattern but you need to choose words with care.

4   Think of other **sequences** or routines. Crossing the road by the Green Cross Code has a sequence. Break up the instructions in the Code into lines so that each line has one command.
    Now write one line of your own to go after each line of the Code. Your lines could be about what you see or hear at a particular road crossing.
    Try a similar routine for:
        cleaning your teeth, laying the table, coming home from school, eating breakfast.

▶   **Sequences** is a particularly good technique for small groups to use. The class can make up a *School Day* poem with different groups working on different parts of the day, or a *School Trip* poem, or a *Journey to P.E.* poem.

Wordplay

Squishy Words

(to be said when 'wet')

SQUIFF
SQUIDGE
SQUAMOUS
SQUINNY
SQUELCH
SQUASH
SQUEEGEE
SQUIRT
SQUAB

Alastair Reid

Seasons

Spring: Slippy, drippy, nippy.
Summer: Showery, flowery, bowery.
Autumn: Hoppy, croppy, poppy.
Winter: Wheezy, sneezy, breezy.

Sydney Smith

GIANTS

THE FLESHLUMPEATER
THE BONECRUNCHER
THE MANHUGGER
THE CHILDCHEWER
THE MEATDRIPPER
THE GIZZARDGULPER
THE MAIDMASHER
THE BLOODBOTTLER
THE BUTCHER BOY

Roald Dahl

The Names of the Months

Jaguary
Cassowary
Marten
Mandrill
Maybird
Coon
Shoofly
Locust
Serpent bear
Octopus
North Pole bear
Remem bear

Christian Morgenstern
German poem translated by Max Knight

FREE SOAP, BLEACH AND DRY
Wednesday FOR BLANKETS
Thursday FOR OLD AGE PENSIONERS

Toilets

Unsuitable for Motor Coaches

HORNETS

Fishermen

Hiyamac.
Lobuddy.
Binearlong?
Cuplours.
Ketchanenny?
Goddafew.
Kindarthay?
Bassencarp.
Enysizetoum?
Cuplapowns.
Hittinard?
Sordalite.
Wahchoozin?
Gobbawurms.
Fishanonaboddum?
Rydonnaboddum.
Igoddago.
Tubad.
Seeyaround.
Yeatakideezy.
Guluk.

Anonymous

League Division Fun

Here are the football results:
League Division Fun
Manchester United won, Manchester City lost
Crystal Palace 2, Buckingham Palace 1

Millwall Leeds nowhere
Wolves 8 A cheese roll and had a cup of tea 2
Aldershot 3 Buffalo Bill shot 2
Evertonill, Liverpool's not very well either
Newcastle's Heaven Sunderland's a very nice place 2
Ipswich one? You tell me.

Michael Rosen

Mean Song

Snickles and podes,
Ribble and grodes:
That's what I wish you.

A nox in the groot,
A root in the stoot
And a gock in the forbeshaw too.

Keep out of sight
For fear that I might
Glom you a gravely snave.

Don't show your face
Around any place
Or you'll get one flack snack in the bave.

Eve Merriam

Eye Sore

I saw
a building
soar
into the sky

making
the sky's
eye
sore.

Roger McGough

I was sitting in the sitting room

I was sitting in the sitting room
toying with some toys
when from a door marked: 'GRUESOME'
There came a GRUESOME noise.

Cautiously I opened it
and there to my surprise
a little GRUE lay sitting
with tears in its eyes.

'Oh little GRUE please tell me
what is it ails thee so?'
'Well I'm so small,' he sobbed,
'GRUESSES don't want to know.'

'Exercises are the answer,
Each morning you must DO SOME.'
He thanked me, smiled,
and do you know what?
The very next day he . . .

Roger McGough

I'll take The High Road Commission

In between the route marks
And the shaving rhymes,
Black and yellow markers
Comment on the times.

All along the highway
Hear the signs discourse:

MEN
SLOW
WORKING

;

SADDLE
CROSSING
HORSE

.

Cryptic crossroad preachers
Proffer good advice,
Helping wary drivers
Keep out of Paradise.

Transcontinental sermons,
Transcendental talk:

SOFT
CAUTION
SHOULDERS

;

CROSS
CHILDREN
WALK

.

Wisest of their proverbs,
Truest of their talk,
Have I found that dictum:

CROSS
CHILDREN
WALK

.

When Adam took the highway
He left his sons a guide:

CROSS
CHILDREN
WALK

;

CHEERFUL
CHILDREN
RIDE

.

Ogden Nash

Zebra Crossing

There is a Lollipopman
At the zebra crossing
With lollipops
He is trying
To lure zebras across
He makes me cross.
I cross.

Roger McGough

Timely

Was an if upon a stair
met a when without a where.
Perhaps hopping up met down
over under through the town.
Nearly backwards inwards fell
to and fro and rang the bell.
All about and round and round
forwards upwards without sound.
Maybe has been lately said
early after soon to bed.

Barbara Giles

In a Word

Sun –
        In a word –
                beams
Rain –
        A green bird –
                drops
Snow –
        White and furred –
                flakes
Thunder –
        All heard –
                claps
Applause, applause, applause,
        Because
Something's always happening
        In a word.

Norman Nicholson

Wordplay

SQUINNY and SQUEEGEE   SLIPPY   DRIPPY   NIPPY

THE GIZZARDGULPER and   I might GLOM you a
THE MAIDMASHER   GRAVELY SNAVE

MANCHESTER UNITED ONE   MANCHESTER CITY LOST

JAGUARY   CASSOWARY   MARTEN

Cross	Cheerful
CHILDREN	CHILDREN
Walk	Ride

Poets are here playing with the sounds and the meanings of words.

1 Find, or make up, words you might say when you are:
   excited   frightened   cold   bored   very happy
   stuck for something to write
   Find, or make up, words to express the sounds of:
   a dripping tap   kicking dead leaves   spilling jelly
   speaking with your mouth full   chips frying
   a full crisp packet   an empty crisp packet
   Find, or make up, words for a sequence like *Names of the Months* (page 33):
   days of the week   months   seasons   numbers
   football teams   relations
   Find, or make up, names like Roald Dahl's list of *Giants* (page 32) for:
   dragons   whales   monsters   teachers
   Find, or make up, words that bring out the sounds of:
   the sea-side   fireworks   breakfast   a building site   roadworks
   a railway station   a busy street

2 In *Mean Song* (page 34) what do you think the poet is actually hoping will
   happen? Try and write a verse which has made-up words to:
   wish someone pleasant things   describe drinking hot soup
   describe having a bath   describe playing in mud in boots

3 Write your own set of Football Results, using the names of some different
   teams but playing with the sounds of the names, as Michael Rosen does
   (page 34).

4 Like *gruesome* in *I was sitting in the sitting room* (page 35) see if you can write a
   poem around words like:
   lonesome (loan some)   porous (poor us)
   juicy (do you see?)   frighten (fry ten)

Conversations

Ghosts

That's right. Sit down and talk to me.
What do you want to talk about?

Ghosts. You were saying that you believe in them.
Yes, they exist, without a doubt.

What, bony white nightmares that rattle and glow?
No, just spirits that come and go.

I've never heard such a load of rubbish.
Never mind, one day you'll know.

What makes you so sure?

I said:
What makes you so sure?

Hey,
Where did you go?

Kit Wright

Which ?

'What did you say?'
'I? Nothing.' 'No? . . .
What was that sound?'
   'When?'
   'Then.'
   'I do not know.'
'Whose eyes were those on us?'
   'Where?'
   'There.'
   'No eyes I saw.'
'Speech, footfall, presence – how cold the night may be!'
'Phantom or fantasy, it's all one to *me*.'

Walter de la Mare

No buts

    'But Dad'.
'No buts Andy you're going if you like it or not!'
    'But . . .'
'Look you're coming and that's that!'
    'But I've got my homework to do . . .'
'You can do that when you get home!'
    'But Dad!'
'No buts son you're coming no matter what you say'.
    'Oh alright Dad'.
'That's better son'.

Elaine Slater

What's the matter up there?

'What's the matter up there?'
'Playing soldiers'
'But soldiers don't make that kind of noise'
'We're playing the kind of soldier that
makes that kind of noise.'

Carl Sandburg

The Leader

I wanna be the leader
I wanna be the leader
Can I be the leader?
Can I? I can?
Promise? Promise?
Yippee, I'm the leader
I'm the leader

OK what shall we do?

Roger McGough

41

All for an ice-cream

'Mum, can I have an ice-cream?'
'Go ask your dad.'
'Dad, can I have an ice-cream?'
'Go ask your mum.'
'But I've just asked her and she told me to ask
  you.'
'Well tell her that I've told you to ask her.'
'Mum, Dad's just told me to tell you that you've
  got to tell me if I can have an ice.'
'Oh well I suppose you can but go ask your dad
  for 10p.'
'Right.'
'Dad, can I have 10p for an ice-cream?'
'I haven't got 10p.'
'Oh come on Dad you haven't looked yet and oh
  hurry the van'll go soon.'
'Let's have a look then, ah, there you are.'
'Thanks Dad, Ohh!'
'What's matter now?'
'The van's gone.'

Karen Jackson

The Crunch

The lion and his tamer
They had a little tiff,
For the lion limped too lamely, –
The bars had bored him stiff.

No need to crack your whip, Sir!
Said the lion then irate:
No need to snap my head off,
Said the tamer – but too late.

Gerda Mayer

I'm the youngest in our house

I'm the youngest in our house
so it goes like this:

My brother comes in and says:
'Tell him to clear the fluff
out from under his bed.'
Mum says,
'Clear the fluff
out from under your bed.'
Father says,
'You heard what your mother said.'
'What?' I say.
'The fluff,' he says.
'Clear the fluff
out from under your bed.'
So I say,
'There's fluff under his bed, too,
you know.'
So father says,
'But we're talking about the fluff
under *your* bed '
'You will clear it up
won't you?' Mum says.
So now my brother – all puffed up –
says,
'Clear the fluff
out from under your bed,
clear the fluff
out from under your bed.'
Now I'm angry. I am angry.
So I say – what shall I say?
I say,
'Shuttup Stinks
YOU CAN'T RULE MY LIFE.'

Michael Rosen

The Ghost

'Who knocks?' 'I, who was beautiful,
   Beyond all dreams to restore,
I, from the roots of the dark thorn am hither,
   And knock on the door.'

'Who speaks?' 'I – once was my speech
   Sweet as the bird's on the air.
When echo lurks by the waters to heed;
   'Tis I speak thee fair.'

'Dark is the hour!' 'Ay, and cold.'
   'Lone is my house.' 'Ah, but mine?'
'Sight, touch, lips, eyes yearned in vain.'
   'Long dead these to thine. . . .'

Silence. Still faint on the porch
   Broke the flames of the stars.
In gloom groped a hope-wearied hand
   Over keys, bolts, and bars.

A face peered. All the grey night
   In chaos of vacancy shone;
Nought but vast sorrow was there –
   The sweet cheat gone.

Walter de la Mare

Conversations

Conversations can give you a natural pattern for a poem. The simplest pattern is the one in *Ghosts* (page 40) where two people are talking in alternate lines. You could call this pattern ABAB. The writer of this poem has taken a well-known 'Doctor, Doctor' joke:
> 'Doctor, doctor, I keep thinking I'm invisible.'
> 'Who said that?'

and turned it into a **conversation poem**.

The poems in this section all have a conversation pattern and have carefully chosen words. *What's the matter up there?* (page 41) gives us a picture of family life. *The Crunch* (page 42) is an example of **wordplay**.

1   People in cartoons have talk-bubbles or think-bubbles.
    Use talk-bubbles to make a **word-shapes conversation poem**.

2   Think of a time when you have had a row with someone and then gone to your room and rewritten the scene in your head so that you win the argument easily. Use a conversation you have had or one you have overheard and improve it so that it makes a **conversation poem**.

3   Listen to the strange things people *really* say: 'don't snap my head off', 'he had eyes as big as saucers', 'the burglars turned the room upside down', 'it made my hair stand on end'. *The Crunch* (page 42) uses one of these sayings. Write a **conversation poem** that takes one of them literally.

4   Write a **conversation**:
        between you and a parent
        between you and a brother or sister
    that will create a picture of family life.

5   Create a picture of school life with a **conversation**:
        between you and a teacher   in the playground   on the bus

6   Many proverbs have opposites:
        Look before you leap.   He who hesitates is lost.
        Many hands make light work.   Too many cooks spoil the broth.
    Choose a proverb and write a **conversation poem**.

Colours

Colours

White's clean and cold
Grey's dusty and dead
Yellow's sunshine and daffodils
Blue's sleep and the sky
Red's for pain.
Red's pricked fingers and scrapes and wounds.

Leon Garfield

Red and White

Nobody picks a red rose when the winter wind howls and the
    white snow blows among the fences and storm doors.
Nobody watches the dreamy sculptures of snow when the summer
    roses blow red and soft in the garden yards and corners.

O I have loved red roses and O I have loved white snow –
    dreamy drifts winter and summer – roses and snow.

Carl Sandburg

What is Pink?

What is pink? A rose is pink
By the fountain's brink.
What is red? A poppy's red
In its barley bed.
What is blue? The sky is blue
Where the clouds float through.
What is white? A swan is white
Sailing in the light.
What is yellow? Pears are yellow,
Rich and ripe and mellow.
What is green? The grass is green,
With small flowers between.
What is violet? Clouds are violet
In the summer twilight.
What is orange? Why, an orange,
Just an orange!

Christina Rossetti

Monday

Moon's Day: the first day
Ought to shine in the week like
New minted silver.

Dull copper thoughts just
Add another penny to
Yesterday's small change.

Michael Richards

Colour Dream

The crimson lakes
   babbled in
the cold
     sun while
the blue moss
   saturated by
the   light
   rain
squelched under
      the strain
  of
tiny green
   roots
The orange trees
   whistled in
the breeze
     and their sooty
     leaves fell in a
heap
  to the
  ground
A yellow zebra
  bounded into
view
  followed by
  a purple lion
Through the
  red bracken
they hurled
    themselves
    to awake
on the verge
  of the crimson
lake.

Patricia Lloyd

Green Winter

A green winter, snow
in some ditches though stubbornly lingers,
very first primroses show,
grass pushes up new fingers,
window-panes carved still with frost triangles,
from branch to branch chaffinches flit,
here and there a catkin dangles,
and every blue and long-tailed tit
pretends to be a clown,
pecking at rind and nut,
viewing the garden upside down,
ice splinters now in each water-butt.

Then suddenly overnight
The golden surprise of one aconite.

Leonard Clark

The Colourblind Birdwatcher

In sallow summer
The loud-mouthed birds
Peer through my hedges
As brown as swallows.

In an acrid autumn
High-flying birds
Splay in formation
As brown as magpies.

In the wan winter
Audacious birds
Besiege my windows
As brown as robins.

In sepia spring
The punctual birds
Resume their habits
As brown as blossom.

U. A. Fanthorpe

Grey

Grey is the sky, and grey the woodman's cot
With grey smoke tumbling from the chimney-pot.
The flagstones are grey that lead to the door;
Grey is the hearth, and grey the worn old floor.

The old man by the fire nods in his chair;
Grey are his clothes and silvery grey his hair.
Grey are the shadows around him creeping,
And grey the mouse from the corner peeping.

James Reeves

Silver

Slowly, silently, now the moon
Walks the night in her silver shoon;
This way, and that, she peers, and sees
Silver fruit upon silver trees;
One by one the casements catch
Her beams beneath the silvery thatch;
Couched in his kennel, like a log,
With paws of silver sleeps the dog;
From their shadowy cote the white breasts peep
Of doves in a silver-feathered sleep;
A harvest mouse goes scampering by,
With silver claws, and silver eye;
And moveless fish in the water gleam,
By silver reeds in a silver stream.

Walter de la Mare

Bronze and Silver

Look
Where the land lies,
Open like a book
Beneath these evening skies;
Still and clear
The stars of September appear,
One by shimmering one,
The bronze day done.

Listen
How the birds sing
When dew drops glisten,
The morning skies murmuring;
Soft and clear
The songs of September appear,
One by trembling one,
The silver day begun.

Leonard Clark

Star Silver

The silver of one star
Plays cross-lights against pine green.

And the play of this silver
Crosswise against the green
Is an old story . . .
                        thousands of years.

And sheep raisers on the hills by night
Watching the woolly four-footed ramblers,
Watching a single silver star –
Why does the story never wear out?

And a baby slung in a feed-box
Back in a barn in a Bethlehem slum,
A baby's first cry mixing with the crunch
Of a mule's teeth on Bethlehem Christmas corn,
Baby fists softer than snowflakes of Norway,
The vagabond Mother of Christ
And the vagabond men of wisdom,
All in a barn on a winter night,
And a baby there in swaddling clothes on hay –
Why does the story never wear out?

The sheen of it all
Is a star silver and a pine green
For the heart of a child asking a story,
The red and hungry, red and hankering heart
Calling for cross-lights of silver and green.

Carl Sandburg

Snow-Buck

They were hunting in a lean time
for magic. The frost had fled the unicorns
further south; white harts built branchy igloos
and teal snoozed under snow.

The albino buck rabbit had grown over clever,
found a way into the garden
where the soft hens might not go;
found remnants of kale, memories of lettuce.

The night he discovered the field gate
they had come down from the forest
under Orion. White horses, gold hawks
hooded on their green wrists.

They went silently, except
for the eagerness of the hounds.
The buck went out in the sugary snow,
rose-eyes lamping in the starlight.

Scenting they began their running.
Over the snow the snow-buck running:
heartbeats sobbing, tracks twisting,
the air fanged with falcons – the catching.

The white buck rabbit disappeared for a year
and a day. Other similar white rabbits
were seen in the Spring,
impossible to catch; canny, green-eyed.

He came back quietly into the garden,
sleek and strong. The family thought at first
he wore a ruby collar – but it was just
a skein of rose-hips, to match his eyes.

Rose Flint

Colour

Yellow is sunshine and
   daffodils

What is pink? A rose is pink
By the fountain's brink

Dull copper thoughts

as brown as blossom

Grey is the sky and grey the
   woodman's cot
With grey smoke tumbling
   from the chimney pot.

This way and that she peers,
   and sees
Silver fruit upon silver trees.

Colourful descriptions make things easier and clearer to see.

1   Write your own:
    'White is . . .
    Grey is . . . like *Colours* (page 46).

2   What **colours** would you use to describe a picture or scene which was:
       frightening   exciting   dull   happy
       sad   mysterious   comfortable?

3   Imagine and then describe a scene which involves lots of different **colours**:
       a fairground   a garden   a decorated Christmas Tree
       a street market   a supermarket

4   We talk of people being:
    green with jealousy, scarlet with embarrassment, in a black mood, having
    green fingers. If people changed **colour**, what would they be like?
    The Blue Girl (in winter)
    The Green Man   The Scarlet Boy – these could be titles of poems.

▶   Collect some household paint cards. Make a **found poem** (page 24) from the
    names for the paints. Use some of the names as starting points for a **colour**
    poem.

▶   Write a class poem on a **colour**. Everyone writes a line beginning with the
    same colour. Collect up the lines and arrange them in verses. Start each
    verse with the colour:
       Grey is Monday on the way to school
       It is the washing in town gardens
       It is the bus tickets in the gutter
       It is the faces of people hurrying to work.

Images

Cleaning Ladies

Belly stuffed with dust and fluff,
   The Hoover moos and drones,
Grazing down on the carpet pasture:
   Cow with electric bones.

Up in the tree of a chair the cat
   Switches off its purr,
Stretches, blinks: a neat pink tongue
   Vacuum-cleans its fur.

Kit Wright

Flashlight

My flashlight tugs me
through the dark
like a hound
with a yellow eye,

sniffs
at the edges
of steep places,

paws
at moles'
and rabbits'
holes,
points its nose
where sharp things
lie asleep –

and then it bounds
ahead of me
on home ground.

Judith Thurman

Yes

YES is a green word,
It grows like grass
It's as crinkly as cabbage,
It's as lush as lime
As springy as sprouts,
It's as lollopy as lettuce
As playful as peas
As artistic as apples,
Yes is as lazy as summer leaves
It's even as squelchy as a fist full of slime.

Frank Flynn

Spring Trees

In the spring when they made the new trees,
They hung up the leaves,
Put fresh bark on the sycamores,
And changed the antifreeze.

Spring made them so carefree
That they strung leaves on a lamp post
And wrapped bark around it.
But later they saw they had barked up the wrong tree.

Sarah Lawson

Boredom

Boredom
Is
Me
Gloomy as Monday
Moidering the time away
Murdering the holiday
Just
Sort of waiting.

Boredom
Is
Clouds
Black as old slate
Chucking rain straight
On our Housing Estate
All grey
Day long.

Boredom
Is
John
In bed again
The trickle of rain
On the window pane
And no one
To play with.

Boredom
Is
Trev
Gone for the day
To Colwyn Bay
For a holiday
And me
On my own.

Boredom
Is
My comics all read
The Library closed
Damp clothes before the fire
Deciding
Not to clean my bike
To tidy my room
To help with washing

Boredom
Is
Empty streets
And black telegraph poles
A muddy tractor
On the building site
Shipwrecked in mud

Boredom
Is
A thick circle
Of emptiness
Heaviness
Nothingness
With me
Slumped in the middle

Boredom
Is
Boredom
Boredom is
Boredom
Is
Boredom

Boredom is
Boredom
Is
Boredom
Boredom is
Boredom
Is
Boredom
Boredom is

Boredom
Is
Boredom
Boredom is
Boredom
Is
Boredom
Boredom is
Boredom
Is
Boredom
Boredom is
Boredom
Is

Gareth Owen

The Squid

What happy appellations these
Of birds and beasts in companies!
A shrewdness of apes, a sloth of bears,
A skulk of foxes, a husk of hares.
An exaltation 'tis of larks,
And possibly a grin of sharks,
But I declare a squirt of squid
I should not like to be amid.
Skin divers boldly swim through sepia,
But I can think of nothing creepier.

Ogden Nash

An Exultation of Larks

A glint of goldfish
A hover of trout
A smack of jellyfish

A leap of leopards
A tower of giraffes
A crash of rhinoceroses

A skulk of thieves
A saunter of cowboys
A dash of commuters

A pitying of turtle doves
A murmuration of starlings
An exultation of larks

Michael Richards

Road Up

What's wrong with the road?
Why all this hush? –
They've given an anaesthetic
In the lunch-hour rush.

They've shaved off the tarmac
With a pneumatic drill,
And bandaged the traffic
To a dead standstill.

Surgeons in shirt-sleeves
Bend over the patient,
Intent on a major
Operation.

Don't dare sneeze!
Don't dare shout!
The road is having
Its appendix out.

Norman Nicholson

The Writer of This Poem

The writer of this poem
Is taller than a tree
As keen as the North wind
As handsome as can be

As bold as a boxing-glove
As sharp as a nib
As strong as scaffolding
As tricky as a fib

As smooth as a lolly-ice
As quick as a lick
As clean as a chemist-shop
As clever as a $\sqrt{}$

The writer of this poem
Never ceases to amaze
He's one in a million billion
(or so the poem says!)

Roger McGough

In the Kitchen

In the kitchen
After the aimless
Chatter of the plates,
The murmurings of the gas,
The chuckle of the water pipes
And the sharp exchanges
Of knives, forks and spoons,
Comes the serious quiet,
When the sink slowly clears its throat
And you can hear the occasional rumble
Of the refrigerator's tummy
As it digests the cold.

John Cotton

View from a High Chair

Here thump on tray
With mug, and splash
Wet white down there.
The sofa purrs,
The window squeaks.
Bump more with mug
And make voice big
Then she will come,
Sky in the room,
Quiet as a cloud,
Flowers in the sky,
Come down snow-soft
But warm as milk,
Hide all the things
That squint with shine,
That gruff and bite
And want to hurt;
Will swallow us
And taste so sweet
As down we go
To try our feet.

Vernon Scannell

Yarns

> They have yarns
> Of a skyscraper so tall they had to put hinges
> On the two top stories so to let the moon go by,
> Of pancakes so thin they had only one side,
>
> Of the hen laying a square egg and cackling. 'Ouch!' and of hens
>   laying eggs with the dates printed on them,
> Of the ship captain's shadow: it froze to the deck one cold winter
>   night,
>
> Of the sheep counter who was fast and accurate: 'I just count their
>   feet and divide by four,'
> Of the man so tall he must climb a ladder to shave himself,
> Of the runt so teeny-weeny it takes two men and a boy to see him,
>
> Of the old man's whiskers: 'When the wind was with him his
>   whiskers arrived a day before he did,'
> Of the man who killed a snake by putting its tail in its mouth so it
>   swallowed itself,
> Of railroad trains shizzing along so fast they reach the station before
>   the whistle.

Carl Sandburg

Magic

> Through my lens, this greenfly on a rose-leaf
> Becomes in an eye-wink a terrifying monster
> Crouching upon the dark-green leathery surface:
> Beside him shines a bright round bubble of dew.
> How odd, how fearful the world must look to him
> As he stares through *his* lens! He sees my face
> (Forehead and curving nose and one huge eye
> Looming down coldly at him, prying and peering);
> My cat, green-tiger-striped with shadow; and that lizard,
> A sliding pterodactyl, as it passes
> Through the tall, tangled forest of the grasses.

Clive Sansom

Five-inch Tall

I'm five-inch tall.
I dive and crawl
Into the jungle
Of the uncut lawn.
Fawn-coloured stems
Of plate-size daisies
Sway round my head
In a tangle of weed.
A monstrous, pop-eyed,
Dinosaur snail
Stares out from the dome
Of his mobile home,
Leaving a slime-trail
Wide as a drain.
In distant, dark-furred
Thickets of twitch,
A cricket whirs
Like a motor-mower.

I creep from the lower
Foothills of lawn
Into a conifer
Forest of horse-tails,
Where writhing, boa-
constrictor worms
Coil round fern-trunks
Or heave through the soil.
Undaunted, unshaken,
I break from the shade
To a lake of sunlight –
Five-inch tall
And the heir of acres,
With all the walled dukedom
To call my own.

But high on a pear-tree
A pocket falcon,
With bragging, flaunted,
Red-flag breast,
Is poised to strike;
Dives down and pounces –
Grappling-iron talons
And beak like a pike.
Shaken, daunted,
Arms over my chest,
I cringe and turn tail;
Off like a shot
To the vegetable plot,
Helter-skelter for the shelter
Of broccoli and kale;
Yielding the field
To red-rag robin –
For safety is all
When you're five-inch tall.

Norman Nicholson

Wall

The wall walks the fell –
Grey millipede on slow
Stone hooves;
Its slack back followed
At gulleys and grooves,
Or shouldering over
Old boulders

Too big to be rolled away.
Fallen fragments
Of the high crags
Crawl in the walk of the wall.

A dry-stone wall
Is a wall and a wall,
Leaning together

(Cumberland-and-Westmorland
Champion wrestlers),
Creening and weathering,
Flank by flank,
With filling of rubble
Between the two –
A double-rank
Stone dyke:
Flags and through –
stones jutting out sideways,
Like the step of a stile.

A wall walks slowly.
At each give of the ground,
Each creek of the rock's ribs,
It puts its foot gingerly,
Arches its hog-holes,
Lets cobble and knee-joint
Settle and grip.
As the slipping fellside
Erodes and drifts,
The wall shifts with it,
Is always on the move.

They built a wall slowly,
A day a week;
Built it to stand,
But not stand still.
They built a wall to walk.

Norman Nicholson

Images

> Clouds black as old slate   Gloomy as Monday
>
> Quiet as a cloud   Wide as a drain   the word bites like a fish

Words can be used to create pictures or **images** in your mind.
When we say that something is like or similar to something really quite
different, that is a **simile**.

> tractor shipwrecked in mud   tall, tangled forest of the grass
>
> the rind mapped with its crimson stain   the waltzing wasp

These are images too but they are comparing two separate things without
using the words 'like' or 'as'. This kind of image is called a **metaphor**.

Sometimes a metaphor can be stretched or extended over a whole poem.
Flashlight (page 56) compares the torch-beam with a dog.
Road Up (page 60) compares road works with an operation by doctors.
In the Kitchen (page 61) compares the kitchen equipment with the behaviour
of people.
So all these poems use **extended metaphors**.

> clouds chucking rain   the wall walks the fell
>
> The house dreamt   the sink slowly clears its throat

These things – the clouds, the wall, the house, the sink – are described as if
they were human. This kind of image is called **personification**.

Our everyday language is full of similes and metaphors that are 'dead'
because they are so common that they no longer create fresh pictures in our
minds. In *Spring Trees* (page 57) 'barked up the wrong tree' uses the dead
image of 'barking up the wrong tree', meaning making the wrong guess.
Originally this would have created an image of a dog barking at one tree
while a cat smirked in another.

1   *Yarns* (page 62) uses images to make jokes. Each line produces an impossible
or ridiculous picture. Write your own yarns about people who are:
>   fat thin tall short bald hairy friendly unfriendly
>   clever stupid interesting boring

2   *Exultation of Larks* (page 59) uses images to create memorable collective
nouns. Make up collective nouns for:
>   school dinners, packed lunches, trains, joggers, traffic wardens,
>   lollypop ladies, felt tips, poems.
Make up a Collective Zoo, a Collective Alphabet, a Collective Family.

3 *Yes* (page 57) uses living similes. Make up living similes to replace the 'dead' ones in:

      as good as gold   as white as a sheet
      as quick as lightning   as happy as a lark

4 Try an **extended metaphor poem** on:

      the school bus   your classroom   a TV set   a computer
      the dentist's chair   the doctor's waiting room   a supermarket
      a washing machine

   What one thing is it like? How can you show this?

5 Look for examples of **personification** in poems. Think of an abstract idea or some object as if it was a person. How would it behave?
(Monday bangs on my door . . .).
Try:

      Monday   Sunday   love   hate   worry
      happiness   Winter   Christmas   holidays   homework

6 *Magic* (page 62) and *Five-Inch Tall* (page 63) look at things as if they were bigger or smaller. Look around you in your classroom or at home and imagine you are either very big or very small. Describe what you see. If you write your poem with one image on each line it will have a pattern.

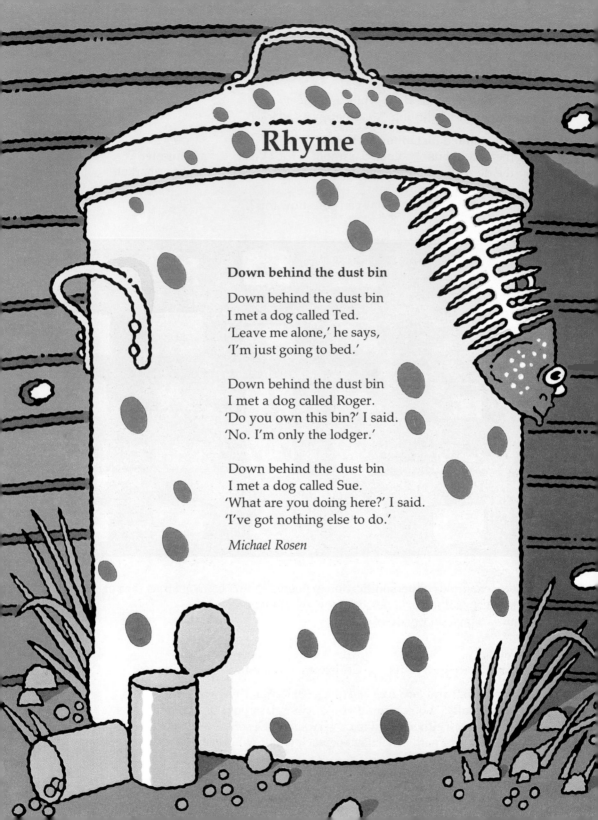

Rhyme

Down behind the dust bin

Down behind the dust bin
I met a dog called Ted.
'Leave me alone,' he says,
'I'm just going to bed.'

Down behind the dust bin
I met a dog called Roger.
'Do you own this bin?' I said.
'No. I'm only the lodger.'

Down behind the dust bin
I met a dog called Sue.
'What are you doing here?' I said.
'I've got nothing else to do.'

Michael Rosen

The Shark

A treacherous monster is the Shark,
He never makes the least remark.

And when he sees you on the sand,
He doesn't seem to want to land.

He watches you take off your clothes,
And not the least excitement shows.

His eyes do not grow bright or roll,
He has astounding self-control.

He waits till you are quite undrest,
And seems to take no interest.

And when towards the sea you leap,
He looks as if he were asleep.

But when you once get in his range,
His whole demeanour seems to change.

He throws his body right about,
And his true character comes out.

It's no use crying or appealing,
He seems to lose all decent feeling.

After this warning you will wish
To keep clear of this treacherous fish.

His back is black, his stomach white,
He has a very dangerous bite.

Lord Alfred Douglas

Habits of the Hippopotamus

The hippopotamus is strong
And huge of head and broad of bustle;
The limbs on which he rolls along
Are big with hippopotomuscle.

He does not greatly care for sweets
Like ice-cream, apple pie, or custard,
But takes to flavour what he eats
A little hippopotomustard.

The hippopotamus is true
To all his principles, and just;
He always tries his best to do
The things one hippopotomust.

He never rides in trucks or trams,
In taxicabs or omnibuses,
And so keeps out of traffic jams
And other hippopotomusses.

Arthur Guiterman

The Cricket

The cricket, like a knuckled rubber-band,
Whirrs from the launching platform of my hand
Without much notion where he's going to land.

But does he mind the jump or the surprise?
Suppose we chanced to be each other's size?
I know I wouldn't stay. I'd close my eyes

And jump. Are bodies chosen with a pin?
My own seems suitable for being in,
But why pale pink, rather than pale green skin?

And does some giant, wishing me no harm,
Peruse me, perfect, on his unseen palm?
What creatures stir upon the cricket's arm?

The worlds are gears upon the wheels of chance.
The worlds retreat and worlds in worlds advance.
The creatures dance. And lead themselves a dance.

Leaping the grasses like a leafy lancer,
The cricket does not know that he's a dancer.
I ask the questions, but he *is* the answer

And all the summer's day he needn't think
But simply jump, a jointed tiddlewink,
A perfect alpha minus in green ink.

John Fuller

The Quarrel

My nostrils are narrowing,
your eyes are staring,
it's terribly harrowing,
there's shouting and swearing,
the bad words are arrowing
to hurting and hearing!

My patience is going,
your anger's increasing,
your glances are glowing,
there's noise without ceasing,
a stormcock is crowing
a storm of releasing!

My fury is creaming,
no thought of the neighbours
restrains your high screaming,
it's childbirth and labours,
a nightmare we're dreaming –
but sharper than sabres!

Gavin Ewart

She is Far from the Land

Cables entangling her,
Shipspars for mangling her,
Ropes, sure of strangling her,
Blocks over-dangling her;
Tiller to batter her,
Topmast to shatter her,
Tobacco to spatter her;
Boreas blustering,
Boatswain quite fustering,
Thunder-clouds mustering
To blast her with sulphur –
If the deep don't engulf her;
Sometimes fear's scrutiny
Pries out a mutiny,
Sniffs conflagration,
Or hints at starvation: –
All the sea-dangers,
Buccaneers, rangers,

Pirates and Salle-men,
Algerine galleymen,
Tornadoes and typhons,
And horrible syphons,
And submarine travels
Thro' roaring sea-navels,
Everything wrong enough,
Long-boat not long enough,
Vessel not strong enough;
Pitch marring frippery,
The deck very slippery,
And the cabin – built sloping,
The Captain a-toping,
And the mate a blasphemer,
That names his Redeemer,
With inward uneasiness;
The cook known by greasiness,
The victuals beslubber'd,

Her bed – in a cupboard;
Things of strange christening,
Snatched in her listening,
Blue lights and red lights
And mention of dead-lights,
And shrouds made a theme of,
Things horrid to dream of, –
And *buoys* in the water,
To fear all exhort her;
Her friend no Leander,
Herself no sea-gander,
And ne'er a cork jacket
On board of the packet!
The breeze still a-stiffening,
The trumpet quite deafening;
Thoughts of repentance,
And Doomsday and sentence;
Everything sinister,

Not a church minister, –
Pilot a blunderer,
Coral reefs under her,
Ready to sunder her;
Trunks tipsy-topsy,
The ship in a dropsy;
Waves oversurging her,
Sirens a-dirgeing her;
Sharks all expecting her,
Swordfish dissecting her,
Crabs with their hand-vices
Punishing land vices;
Sea-dogs and unicorns,
Things with no puny horns,
Mermen carnivorous –
'Good Lord deliver us!'

Thomas Hood

Rhyme-Time

I know that poems do not have to rhyme,
And yet I've always liked to hear words chime.
I've noticed, too, that in the world's design
Rhymes play their part, occurring all the time,
Not just in sounds but in the way the fine
Gestures of a tiny plant will mime
In miniature the flourish of a pine,
Proud and lonely on the hill's skyline;
Or how the bright refulgence of moonshine
Is almost echoed in the sheen of lime;
The way the hawthorn foams, a paradigm
For spindrift blossom on the dancing brine.
Oh yes, it's true, all poems do not rhyme
But of the things that I will treasure, nine
Times out of ten, the sounds and objects sign
Themselves on memory and warmly twine
Around the heart and rhythms of the spine
Through using chime and echo.
                                        It's no crime –
As verbal savages in grime and slime
Of their poetic darkness whine – to climb
To transcendental heights or try to mine
Deep in mysteries equally sublime
By rungs or shafts of rhyme. I know that I'm
Old fashioned but I'd never care to sign
A contract that debars the chiming line.
Finally, I ask, what sweeter rhyme
Than your close heartbeat keeping time with mine?

Vernon Scannell

Rhyme

rhyming couplets	A treacherous monster is the *Shark*	**A**
	He never makes the least *remark*	**A**
	And when he sees you on the *sand*	**B**
	He doesn't seem to want to *land*.	**B**
rhyming triplets	The cricket, like a knuckled rubber-*band*	**A**
	Whirrs from the launching platform of my *hand*	**A**
	Without much notion where he's going to *land*	**A**

The hippopotamus is
strong   **A**
And huge of head and broad
of *bustle*;   **B**
The limbs on which he rolls
along   **A**
Are big with hippopoto
muscle.   **B**

Down behind the dust
bin   **A**
I met a dog called *Ted*.   **B**
'Leave me alone,' he
says   **C**
'I'm just going to *bed*.'   **B**

As you will have seen from many of the poems already, rhyme is not
necessary for a poem; but a rhyme scheme, like those here, can help to
give the verses pattern.

1 Try writing a **rhyming couplet** about:
    a bus   a worm   a crash
    mud   a fish
or any other object you can think of. See if you can expand some of your
rhyming couplets now to **triplets**.

The next stage is to have lines rhyming alternately (ABAB), as in *The Quarrel*
and *Habits of the Hippopotamus*. What other poems can you find in the book
which rhyme in this way? Choose any subject and try to use rhyme like this.

2 Michael Rosen, who wrote the verses *Down behind the dust bin* (page 68) also
has verses about dogs called:
Felicity   Anne   Jack   Jim   Billy   Barry   Mary
Can you imagine how he writes the third and fourth lines for them, with an
ABCB rhyme-scheme?

Try some more with other names you can think of; you can also try to
improve on the three in the book.

3 Vernon Scannell, see *Rhyme-Time* (opposite), obviously worked hard at
finding as many words as he could to rhyme with rhyme'. Take a word like
'round', 'last', fling', 'take' and make a list of words which rhyme with each
of them. Then see if you can make one set of rhyming words into a poem.

Ballads

The Enchanted Shirt

The King was sick. His cheek was red,
  And his eye was clear and bright;
He ate and drank with a kingly zest,
  And peacefully snored at night.

But he said he was sick, and a king should know,
  And doctors came by the score;
They did not cure him. He cut off their heads,
  And sent to the schools for more.

At last two famous doctors came,
  And one was as poor as a rat;
He had passed his life in studious toil,
  And never found time to grow fat.

The other had never looked in a book;
  His patients gave him no trouble;
If they recovered they paid him well,
  If they died their heirs paid double.

Together they looked at the royal tongue,
  As the King on his couch reclined;
In succession they thumped his august chest,
  But no trace of disease could find.

The old sage said, 'You're as sound as a nut.'
  'Hang him up!' roared the king, in a gale –
In a ten-knot gale – of royal rage.
  The other leech grew a shade pale.

But he pensively rubbed his sagacious nose,
  And thus his prescription ran –
The King will be well if he sleeps one night
  In the shirt of a happy man.

Wide o'er the realm the couriers rode,
    And fast their horses ran;
And many they saw, and to many they spoke,
    But they found no happy man.

*   *   *

At last they came to a village gate,
    A beggar lay whistling there;
He whistled and sang and laughed and rolled
    On the grass in the soft June air.

The weary courtiers paused and looked
    At the scamp so blithe and gay;
And one of them said, 'Heaven save you, friend,
    You seem to be happy today.'

'O yes, fair sirs!' the rascal laughed,
    And his voice rang free and glad;
'An idle man has so much to do
    That he never has time to be sad.'

'This is our man,' the courtier said;
    'Our luck has led us aright;
I will give you a hundred ducats, friend,
    For the loan of your shirt tonight.'

The merry blackguard lay back on the grass,
    And laughed till his face was black;
'I would do it, God wot,' and he roared with the fun,
    'But I haven't a shirt to my back.'

John Hay

The Housewife's Lament

One day I was walking, I heard a complaining
And saw an old woman the picture of gloom.
She gazed at the mud on her doorstep, 'twas raining,
And this was her song as she wielded her broom.

O life is a toil, and love is a trouble.
Beauty will fade and riches will flee.
Pleasures they dwindle and prices they double
And nothing is as I would wish it to be.

There's too much of worriment goes to a bonnet,
There's too much of ironing goes to a shirt,
There's nothing that pays for the time that you
   waste on it,
There's nothing that lasts but trouble and dirt.

In March it is mud, it is slush in December,
The mid-summer breezes are loaded with dust.
In fall the leaves litter, in muddy September
The wallpaper rots and the candlesticks rust.

It's sweeping at six and it's dusting at seven.
It's victuals at eight and it's dishes at nine.
It's potting and panning from ten to eleven,
We've scarce finished breakfast, we're ready to dine.

Last night in my dreams I was stationed forever
On a far little rock in the midst of the sea.
My one chance of life was a ceaseless endeavour
To sweep off the waves as they swept over me.

Alas! 'Twas no dream; ahead I behold it,
I see I am helpless my fate to avert.
She lay down her broom, her apron she folded,
She lay down and died, and was buried in dirt.

Anonymous

78

As I walked out in the streets of Laredo

As I walked out in the streets of Laredo,
As I walked out in Laredo one day,
I spied a poor cowboy wrapped up in white linen,
Wrapped up in white linen as cold as the clay.

'I see by your outfit that you are a cowboy,'
These words he did say as I boldly stepped by.
'Come, sit down beside me and hear my sad story;
I was shot in the breast and I know I must die.

Once in my saddle I used to look handsome,
Once in my saddle I used to look gay.
I first went to drinkin 'and then to card playin',
Got shot in the breast, which ended my day.

Let sixteen gamblers come handle my coffin,
Let sixteen girls come carry my pall;
Put bunches of roses all over my coffin,
Put roses to deaden the clods as they fall.

And beat the drums slowly and play the fife lowly,
And play the dead march as you carry me along;
Take me to the prairie and lay the sod o'er me,
For I'm a young cowboy and I know I've done wrong.'

We beat the drums slowly and played the fife lowly,
And bitterly wept as we bore him along;
For we all loved our comrade so brave, young and handsome,
We loved the young cowboy although he'd done wrong.

Anonymous

RABBIT IN MIXER SURVIVES

A baby rabbit fell into a quarry's mixing machine yesterday and came out in the middle of a concrete block. But the rabbit still had the strength to dig its way free before the block set.

The tiny creature was scooped up with 30 tons of sand, then swirled and pounded through the complete mixing process. Mr Michael Hooper, the machine operator, found the rabbit shivering on top of the solid concrete block, its coat stiff with fragments. A hole from the middle of the block and paw marks showed the escape route.

Mr Reginald Denslow, manager of J. R. Pratt and Sons' quarry at Kilmington, near Axminster, Devon, said: 'This rabbit must have a lot more than nine lives to go through this machine. I just don't know how it avoided being suffocated, ground, squashed or cut in half.' With the 30 tons of sand, it was dropped into a weighing hopper and carried by conveyor to an overhead mixer where it was whirled around with gallons of water.

From there the rabbit was swept to a machine which hammers wet concrete into blocks by pressure of 100 lb per square inch. The rabbit was encased in a block eighteen inches long, nine inches high and six inches thick. Finally the blocks were ejected on to the floor to dry and the dazed rabbit clawed itself free. 'We cleaned him up, dried him by the electric fire, then he hopped away,' Mr Denslow said.

Daily Telegraph

'Tell us a story Grandad'
The bunny rabbits implored
'About the block of concrete
Out of which you clawed.'

'Tell every gory detail
Of how you struggled free
From the teeth of the Iron Monster
And swam through a quicksand sea.'

'How you battled with the Humans
(And the part we like the most)
Your escape from the raging fire
When they held you there to roast.'

The old adventurer smiled
And waved a wrinkled paw
'All right children, settle down
I'll tell it just once more.'

His thin nose started twitching
Near-blind eyes began to flood
As the part that doesn't age
Drifted back to bunnyhood.

When spring was king of the seasons
And days were built to last
When thunder was merely thunder
Not a distant quarry blast.

How, leaving the warren one morning
Looking for somewhere to play,
He'd wandered far into the woods
And there had lost his way.

When suddenly without warning
The earth gave way, and he fell
Off the very edge of the world
Into the darkness of Hell.

Sharp as the colour of a carrot
On a new-born bunny's tongue
Was the picture he recalled
Of that day when he was young.

Trance-formed now by the memory
His voice was close to tears
But the story he was telling
Was falling on deaf ears.

There was giggling and nudging
And lots of 'sssh – he'll hear'
For it was a trick, a game they played
Grown crueller with each year.

'Poor old Grandad' they tittered
As they one by one withdrew
'He's told it all so often
He now believes it's true.'

Young rabbits need fresh carrots
And his had long grown stale
So they left the old campaigner
Imprisoned in his tale.

Petrified by memories
Haunting ever strong
Encased in a block of time
Eighteen inches long.

* * *

Alone in a field in Devon
An old rabbit is sitting, talking,
When out of the wood, at the edge
of the world,
A man with a gun comes walking.

Roger McGough

81

The Ballad of Billy Rose

Outside Bristol Rovers Football Ground –
The date has gone from me, but not the day,
Nor how the dissenting flags in stiff array
Struck bravely out against the grey sky's round –

Near the Car Park then, past Austin and Ford,
Lagonda, Bentley, and a colourful patch
Of country coaches come in for the match
Was where I walked, having travelled the road

From Fishponds to watch Portsmouth in the Cup.
The Third Round, I believe. And I was filled
With the old excitement which had thrilled
Me so completely when, while growing up,

I went on Saturdays to match or fight.
Not only me; for thousands of us there
Strode forward eagerly, each man aware
Of vigorous memory, anticipating delight.

We all marched forward, all, except one man.
I saw him because he was paradoxically still,
A stone against the flood, face upright against us all,
Head bare, hoarse voice aloft. Blind as a stone.

I knew him at once despite his pathetic clothes;
Something in his stance, or his sturdy frame
Perhaps. I could even remember his name
Before I saw it on his blind-man's tray. Billy Rose.

And twenty forgetful years fell away at the sight.
Bare-kneed, dismayed, memory fled to the hub
Of Saturday violence, with friends to the Labour Club
Watching the boxing on a sawdust summer night.

The boys' enclosure close to the shabby ring
Was where we stood, clenched in a resin world,
Spoke in cool voices, lounged, were artificially bored
During minor bouts. We paid threepence to go in.

Billy Rose fought there. He was top of the bill.
So brisk a fighter, so gallant, so precise!
Trim as a tree he stood for the ceremonies
Then turned to meet George Morgan of Tirphil.

He had no chance. Courage was not enough,
Nor tight defence. Donald Davies was sick –
We threatened his cowardice with an embarrassed kick.
Ripped across both his eyes was Rose, but we were tough

And clapped him as they wrapped his blindness up
In busy towels, applauded the wave
He gave his executioner, cheered the brave
Blind man as he cleared with jaunty hop

The top rope. I had forgotten that day
As if it were dead for ever, yet now I saw
The flowers of punched blood on the ring floor.
As bright as his name. I do not know

How long I stood with ghosts of the wild fists
And the cries of shaken boys long dead around me,
For struck to act at last, in terror and pity
I threw some frantic money, three treacherous pence

(I cry at the memory) into his tray, and ran,
Entering the waves of the stadium like a drowning man.
Poor Billy Rose. God, he could fight
Before my three sharp coins knocked out his sight.

Leslie Norris

Ballads

Ballads are good examples of the regular use of **rhyme**. They also have a regular **rhythm**, which consists of regular 'beats' or stresses in a line:

The Kíng was síck. His chéek was réd,   A
And his éye was cléar and bríght;   B
He áte and dránk with a kíngly zést   C
And peácefully snóred at níght.   B

The lines 1 and 3 have **four** beats, lines 2 and 4 have **three** (4:3:4:3).
This has **four** beats to each line as does *As I walked out in the streets of Laredo* (page 79):

One dáy I was wálking, I heárd a compláining   A
And sáw an old wóman the pícture of glóom.   B
She gázed at the múd on her dóorstep, 'twas ráining   A
And thís was her sóng as she wiélded her bróom.   B

This has **five** beats to each line

Oútside Brístol, Róvers Foótball Gróund   A
The dáte has góne, from me, but nót the dáy   B
Nor hów the dissént
ing flágs in stíff arráy   B
Struck brávely oút agaínst the gréy sky's róund.   A

This has **three** beats to each line:

Téll us a stóry, Grándad,   A
The búnny rábbits implóred   B
Abóut the blóck of cóncrete   C
Oút of whích you cláwed.   B

1   The most common pattern for a ballad is a rhyme scheme of ABCB and a rhythm of 4:3:4:3 beats to a verse of four lines. Think of a story that you know well – make it quite a simple, short one – and try telling it as a ballad.

2   Or you might take a real story from a newspaper or from the TV News and turn it into a story-poem, as Roger McGough did with the story *Rabbit in Mixer Survives* (page 81). Keep to verses of four lines and try to keep the rhythm and the rhyme regular.

3   Write some verses with **three** beats to each line; then try with **four** and even **five**; try to 'hear' the rhythm as you write.

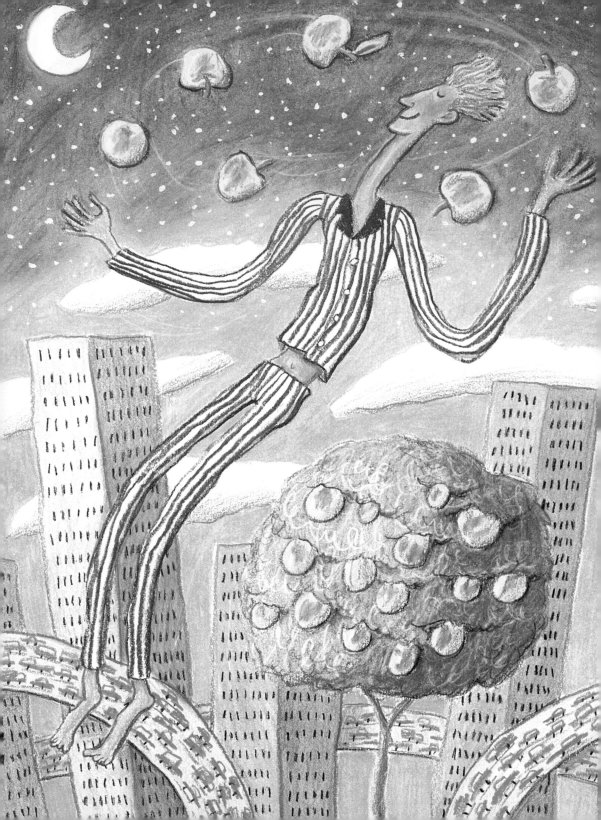

Themes

In this section, different poets have approached the themes of **Sleep, Space, Apples** and **Town Life** in different ways. Explore the sections yourself and see how many approaches there are; then try some of the following suggestions, which are approaches to the same themes which these poets have not tried.

   Choose an idea, choose a pattern for your poem, think of the feelings you want to show, try to use some images. These are ideas for poems, not titles: often the best titles come when the poem is finished.

Sleep
Thoughts in the dark while trying to get to sleep
Dreams and nightmares
Fear of going to sleep
Noises you hear when you are in bed and others are still awake
Waking up – the change from a dream to reality
                    the change from a warm bed to a cold room

Space
Floating in space in a capsule
Floating in space outside a capsule
The view from the capsule window
Your view of the inhabitants of another planet
Their view of you
Re-entry from space – the contrast in surroundings

Apples
From the point of view of one who dislikes apples
Rotten apples
Which apple in the bowl to choose
Different types and colours of apples
On reaching the core
From apple to sauce

Town Life
A town after dark
Playing in the street, in a public playground
The neighbours
Where town stops and country begins
All the different things that make up traffic

This book finishes with some poems written about writing poetry. Every poet takes great thought and care over a finished poem, going over the words and the pattern and the image again and again. Read these poems to yourself: you may well understand some of the feelings, now that you have tried writing some poetry.

Sleep

Bully Night

Bully night
I do not like
the company you keep
The burglars and the bogeymen
who slink
while others sleep

Bully night
I do not like
the noises that you make
The creaking and the shrieking
that keep me
fast awake

Bully night
I do not like
the loneliness you bring
the loneliness you bring
The loneliness, the loneliness
the loneliness you bring,
the loneliness you bring
the loneliness, the

Roger McGough

Good Night

Here's a body – there's a bed!
There's a pillow – here's a head!
There's a curtain – here's a light!
There's a puff – and so good night!

Thomas Hood

Nurse's Song

Sleep, baby, sleep!
Your father herds his sheep:
Your mother shakes the little tree
From which fall pretty dreams on thee;
Sleep, baby, sleep!

Sleep, baby, sleep!
The heavens are white with sheep:
For they are lambs – those stars so bright:
And the moon's shepherd of the night;
Sleep, baby, sleep!

Sleep, baby, sleep!
And I'll give thee a sheep,
Which, with its golden bell, shall be
A little play-fellow for thee;
Sleep, baby, sleep!

Sleep, baby, sleep!
And bleat not like a sheep,
Or else the shepherd's angry dog
Will come and bite my naughty rogue;
Sleep, baby, sleep!

Sleep, baby, sleep!
Go out and herd the sheep,
Go out, you barking black dog, go,
And waken not my baby so;
Sleep, baby, sleep!

Anonymous
(translated from the German)

Caterpillar's Lullaby

Your sleep will be
a lifetime
and all your dreams
rainbows.
Close your eyes
and spin yourself
a fairytale:
Sleeping Ugly,
Waking Beauty.

Jane Yolen

Mother Worm's Hum

Sleep, young wriggler,
Under your grass coverlet,
Under your earth sheet.
Do not be surprised to find
That morning is just as dark.

Jane Yolen

The Troll to her Children

Billy Goat Gruff
Was yesterday's lunch,
So go to sleep fast
Or I'll give you a punch.

Jane Yolen

Mother Owl's Song

Sleep will come
On silent wings
And lead you through the day.
Do not fear the light
For I am by your side.
The sun will not find you
Not eat up
Your predaceous dreams.
Dream, child, of the blood,
The sudden warmth,
And the faltering heartbeat
Beneath your claws.
Dream of the rabbit's scream,
And the frantic scutter
Of mice and mole.
Dream, little one,
Precious mine,
Till night invites you
Out of dreams
And into the hunt once more.

Jane Yolen

Sweet Dreams

I wonder as into bed I creep
What it feels like to fall asleep.
I've told myself stories, I've counted sheep,
But I'm always asleep when I fall asleep.
Tonight my eyes I will open keep,
And I'll stay awake till I fall asleep,
Then I'll know what it feels like to fall asleep,
Asleep,
Asleeep,
Asleeeep . . . . . .

Ogden Nash

To Sleep

A flock of sheep that leisurely pass by,
One after one; the sound of rain and bees
Murmuring; the fall of rivers, winds and seas,
Smooth fields, white sheets of water, and pure sky;
I have thought of all by turns, and yet do lie
Sleepless! and soon the small birds' melodies
Must hear, first uttered from my orchard trees;
And the first cuckoo's melancholy cry.
Even thus last night, and two nights more, I lay
And could not win thee, Sleep! by any stealth:
So do not let me wear tonight away:
Without thee what is all the morning's wealth?
Come, blessed barrier between day and day,
Dear mother of fresh thought and joyous health!

William Wordsworth

Falling Asleep

Voices moving about in the quiet house:
Thud of feet and a muffled shutting of doors:
Everyone yawning. Only the clocks are alert.

Out in the night there's autumn-smelling gloom
Crowded with whispering trees; across the park
A hollow cry of hounds like lonely bells:
And I know that the clouds are moving across the moon;
The low, red, rising moon. Now herons call
And wrangle by their pool; and hooting owls
Sail from the wood above pale stooks of oats.

Waiting for sleep, I drift from thoughts like these;
And where to-day was dream-like; build my dreams.
Music . . . there was a bright white room below,
And someone singing a song about a soldier,
One hour, two hours ago: and soon the song
Will be '*last night*': but now the beauty swings
Across my brain, ghost of remembered chords
Which still can make such radiance in my dream
That I can watch the marching of my soldiers,
And count their faces; faces; sunlit faces.

Falling asleep . . . the herons, and the hounds. . . .
September in the darkness; and the world
I've known; all fading past me into peace.

Siegfried Sassoon

Space

Space Pilot

The land sinks back
The rockets shoot their bolt,
Earth's pull weakens and dies.
I breach space and become a celestial body,
Moving with planets and suns
Through darkness, silence and cold,
But having no place in this void
My weight lost, my breath in an envelope
My eyes replaced by intricate instruments.
There is no place for the heart.
Here, needing the light and the seasons.
But the soul perhaps?
Released from all that I could not carry with me
I shall stare unhindered into the face of God.

John Blackie

The Unending Sky

I could not sleep for thinking of the sky,
   The unending sky, with all its million suns
Which turn their planets everlastingly
   In nothing, where the fire-haired comet runs.
If I could sail that nothing, I should cross
   Silence and emptiness with dark stars passing;
Then, in the darkness, see a point of gloss
   Burn to a glow, and glare, and keep massing,
And rage into a sun with wandering planets,
   And drop behind; and then, as I proceed,
See his last light upon his last moon's granites
   Die to a dark that would be night indeed:
Night where my soul might sail a million years
In nothing, not even Death, not even tears.

John Masefield

The Eagle has Landed

The airlock swings open –
behold! a new world:
obsidian black sky
lit by the sun's
fierce glare.
Inch
down the ladder –
the first man on the moon!
Look!
The first footprint.
Listen!
The first word
splitting the still dead silence.
Dead dust
dead rock
dead black sky.
A dead dead world.
Zombie in a moontrance I
trip
stumble
fall
rise
before the slow dust settles.
I leap in lingering arches.
Steady yourself.
Get your samples –
moondust moonrock.
Temperature check.
Humidity test.
And so
plod
carefully back.
My footprints in the ancient dust.

Adrian Rumble

54321

5
4
3
2
1 rocket
2 the moon
3 flew it
what 4 ?
5
4
3
2

1 rocket

Michael Rosen

Halley's Comet

My father saw it back in 1910,
The year King Edward died.
Above dark telegraph poles, above the high
Spiked steeple of the Liberal Club, the white
Gas-lit dials of the Market Clock,
Beyond the wide
Sunset-glow cirrus of blast-furnace smoke,
My father saw it fly
Its thirty-seven-million-mile-long kite
Across Black Combe's black sky.

And what of me,
Born four years too late?
Will I have breath to wait
Till the long-circuiting commercial traveller
Turns up at his due?
In 1986, aged seventy-two,
Watery in the eyes and phlegmy in the flue
And a bit bad tempered at so delayed a date,
Will I look out above whatever is left of the town –
The Liberal Club long closed and the clock stopped,
And the chimneys smokeless above damped-down
Furnace fires? And then will I
At last have chance to see it
With my own as well as my father's eyes,
And share his long-ago Edwardian surprise
At that high, silent jet, laying its bright trail
Across Black Combe's black sky?

Norman Nicholson

The First Men on Mercury

— We come in peace from the third planet.
Would you take us to your leader?

— Bawr stretter! Bawr. Bawr. Stretterhawl?

— This is a little plastic model
of the solar system, with working parts.
You are here and we are there and we
are now here with you, is this clear?

— Gawl horrop. Bawr. Abawrhannahanna!

— Where we come from is blue and white
with brown, you see we call the brown
here 'land', the blue is 'sea', and the white
is 'clouds' over land and sea, we live
on the surface of the brown land,
all round is sea and clouds. We are 'men'.
Men come —

— Glawp men! Gawrbenner menko. Menhawl?

— Men come in peace from the third planet
which we call 'earth'. We are earthmen.
Take us earthmen to your leader.

— Thmen? Thmen? Bawr. Bawrhossop.
Yuleeda tan hanna. Harrabost yuleeda.

— I am the yuleeda. You see my hands,
we carry no benner, we come in peace.
The spaceways are all stretterhawn.

— Glawn peacemen all horrabhanna tantko!
Tan come at'mstrossop. Glawp yuleeda!

— Atoms are peacegawl in our harraban.
Menbat worrabost from tan hannahanna.

— You men we know bawrhossoptant. Bawr.
We know yuleeda. Go strawg backspetter quick.

— We cantantabawr, tantingko backspetter now!

— Banghapper now! Yes, third planet back.
Yuleeda will go back blue, white, brown
nowhanna! There is no more talk.

— Gawl han fasthapper?

— No. You must go back to your planet.
Go back in peace, take what you have gained
but quickly.

— Stretterworra gawl, gawl . . .

— Of course, but nothing is ever the same,
now is it? You'll remember Mercury.

Edwin Morgan

Off to Outer Space Tomorrow Morning

You can start the Count Down, you can take a last look;
You can pass me my helmet from its plastic hook;
You can cross out my name in the telephone book –
    For I'm off to Outer Space tomorrow morning.

There won't be any calendar, there won't be any clock;
Daylight will be on the switch and winter under lock.
I'll doze when I'm sleepy and wake without a knock –
    For I'm off to Outer Space tomorrow morning.

I'll be writing no letters; I'll be posting no mail.
For with nobody to visit me and not a friend in hail,
In solit'ry confinement as complete as any gaol
    I'll be off to Outer Space tomorrow morning.

When my capsule door is sealed and my space-flight has begun,
With the teacups circling round me like the planets round the sun,
I'll be centre of my gravity, a universe of one,
    Setting off to Outer Space tomorrow morning.

You can watch on television and follow from afar,
Tracking through your telescope my upward shooting star,
But you needn't think I'll give a damn for you or what you are
    When I'm off to Outer Space tomorrow morning.

And when the rockets thrust me on my trans-galactic hop,
With twenty hundred light-years before the first stop,
Then you and every soul on earth can go and blow your top —
    For I'm off to Outer Space tomorrow morning.

Norman Nicholson

Burning Burning Moonward

Burning burning moonward
straight across the sky
deep into the universe
toward the moon on high.

Behind us now in blackness
Earth misty white and blue
lovely and abandoned
breathless bright and new.

Gliding gliding moonward
dancing through a void
turning to the music
of star and asteroid.

Gigantic looming satellite
pocked and cratered crust
silver ashen grey
cold rock and ancient dust.

Falling falling moonward
heart pounding in my chest
hiss of retro fire
and our spacecraft comes to rest.

Adrian Rumble

Spacepoem 3: Off Course

the golden flood   the weightless seat
the cabin song   the pitch black
the growing beard   the floating crumb
the shining rendezvous   the orbit wisecrack
the hot spacesuit   the smuggled mouth-organ
the imaginary somersault   the visionary sunrise
the turning continents   the space debris
the golden lifeline   the space walk
the crawling deltas   the camera moon
the pitch velvet   the rough sleep
the crackling headphone   the space silence
the turning earth   the lifeline continents
the cabin sunrise   the hot flood
the shining spacesuit   the growing moon
the crackling somersault   the smuggled orbit
the rough moon   the visionary rendezvous
the weightless headphone   the cabin debris
the floating lifeline   the pitch sleep
the crawling camera   the turning silence
the space crumb   the crackling beard
the orbit mouth-organ   the floating song

Edwin Morgan

Apples

The Apple's Song

Tap me with your finger,
rub me with your sleeve,
hold me, sniff me, peel me
curling round and round
till I burst out white and cold
from my tight red coat
and tingle in your palm
as if I'd melt and breathe
a living pomander
waiting for the minute
of joy when you lift me
to your mouth and crush me
and in taste and fragrance
I race through your head
in my dizzy dissolve.
I sit in the bowl
in my cool corner
and watch you as you pass
smoothing your apron.
Are you thirsty yet?
My eyes are shining.

Edwin Morgan

Apple Song

I am an apple
I swing on the tree
I have a sharpness
At the heart of me

And no sun at noonday
Brutal with heat
Can utterly tame me
And render me sweet

Don't eat me on picnics
At height of midsummer
With lettuce and radish
Tomatoes, cucumber

When your body is tanned
And your mind thick as cream
And all life a languorous
Strawberry dream

But when Autumn is stirred
By a spoon of a wind
And the clothes you are wearing
Seem suddenly thinned

And your walk through the orchard
Is vaguely beset
By currents of feeling –
Nostalgia, regret,

And you need an assurance
That December and June
Can be blended together,
Pluck me down. Eat me then.

Brian Jones

Moonlit Apples

At the top of the house the apples are laid in rows,
And the skylight lets the moonlight in, and those
Apples are deep-sea apples of green. There goes
A cloud on the moon in the autumn night.

A mouse in the wainscot scratches, and scratches, and then
There is no sound at the top of the house of men
Or mice; and the cloud is blown, and the moon again
Dapples the apples with deep-sea light.

They are lying in rows there, under the gloomy beams;
On the sagging floor; they gather the silver streams
Out of the moon, those moonlight apples of dreams,
And quiet is the steep stair under.

In the corridors under there is nothing but sleep.
And stiller than ever on orchard boughs they keep
Tryst with the moon, and deep is the silence, deep
On moon-washed apples of wonder.

J. Drinkwater

Apples

Behold the apples' rounded worlds:
juice-green of July rain,
the black polestar of flower, the rind
mapped with its crimson stain.

The russet, crab and cottage red
burn to the sun's hot brass,
then drop like sweat from every branch
and bubble in the grass.

They lie as wanton as they fall,
and where they fall and break,
the stallion clamps his crunching jaws,
the starling stabs his beak.

In each plump gourd the cidery bite
of boys' teeth tears the skin;
the waltzing wasp consumes his share,
the bent worm enters in.

I, with as easy hunger, take
entire my season's dole;
welcome the ripe, the sweet, the sour,
the hollow and the whole.

Laurie Lee

After Apple-Picking

My long two-pointed ladder's sticking through a tree
Toward heaven still,
And there's a barrel that I didn't fill
Beside it, and there may be two or three
Apples I didn't pick upon some bough.
But I am done with apple-picking now.
Essence of winter sleep is on the night,
The scent of apples: I am drowsing off.
I cannot rub the strangeness from my sight
I got from looking through a pane of glass
I skimmed this morning from the drinking trough
And held against the world of hoary grass.
It melted, and I let it fall and break.
But I was well
Upon my way to sleep before it fell,
And I could tell
What form my dreaming was about to take.
Magnified apples appear and disappear,
Stem end and blossom end,
And every fleck of russet showing clear.
My instep arch not only keeps the ache,
It keeps the pressure of a ladder-round.
I feel the ladder sway as the boughs bend.
And I keep hearing from the cellar bin
The rumbling sound
Of load on load of apples coming in.
For I have had too much
Of apple-picking: I am overtired
Of the great harvest I myself desired.
There were ten thousand thousand fruit to touch,
Cherish in hand, lift down, and not let fall.
For all
That struck the earth,

No matter if not bruised or spiked with stubble,
Went surely to the cider-apple heap
As of no worth.
One can see what will trouble
This sleep of mine, whatever sleep it is.
Were he not gone,
The woodchuck could say whether it's like his
Long sleep, as I describe its coming on,
Or just some human sleep.

Robert Frost

Apple

When I
bite into
an apple
there is
a squirt
of juice
that hits
me in
my eye,
then
about ten minutes after
I am pulling
the
bits
of
apple
from
between
my
teeth

David Cooper

Applemoon

Something woke me: startle-sound
or moonlight. The house dreamt
like an old cat, but I
looked out my window.

And night was day in a midnight
moon-flood. Mazy moon
flaring a halo of quick clouds
running the big black sky.
And I saw a thousand windfall apples
lying luminous as sea-stones beached
below the spiky silver trees.

So, shivering I
mouse-went out
with a basket, barefoot, toes
curling in the cold;
and singing soft
took ripe reluctant apples
under close and curious stars.

Only soon I saw
my shadow was not
the same as I;
it stooped more –
had its own thinness . . .
and our fingers
never met.

I quick-ran back
the house so
sleepy-warm, sure.
But looking out through curtain lace
I saw my shadow linger
moving slow and crooked, plucking
shadow apples
from the shining moony grass.

Rose Flint

Town and Country

People who live in towns
Often talk to themselves.
They have little sunlight,
Less quiet, and nothing very fresh to eat.
Loving is quite a problem.

Their pleasures are not all that pleasant,
Though they pay dearly for them.
In a dry summer,
Towns smell of money going bad.

Country people have skins like fruit, and vote like grandad.
They treat cattle like cows,
And speak kindly to strangers –
Though they use too many poisons
Which they buy from towns.

Suburban people are different from either.
Bringing up their gardens,
They are kind by committee,
And smile behind gates.
They are not seen talking to themselves.

Town people try very hard
Not to be taken in.
Sometimes they die of not being taken in,
Anywhere by anyone.

The sky grows closer,
The landlords more so,
Chimneys get cleaner,
Green belts blacker.

Gordon Symes

The Romanies in Town

let us leave this place, brother
it is not for us
they have built a great city
with broken glass
see how it shimmers in the evening light?

their feet are bleeding
through walking on splinters
they pretend not to notice

they have offered us a house
with cabbages in the garden
they tell us of their strange country
and want us to stay
and help them fight for it

do not listen, brother
they will bind you with promises
and with hope
on all sides stretch fields of rubble
they say we should admire the view

the young are busy building
new glass palaces
they gather up the splinters
and bathe their feet with tears

come quick come quick
we will take the road towards the sea
we will pick blackberries
from hedges in the lanes
we will pitch camp on empty moors
and watch the hawk skimming
above the trees

but if we do not fight
the hawks will die, sister
they have no time for wild birds
and will shoot us down

Anne Beresford

Out in the City

When you're out in the city
Shuffling down the street,
A bouncy city rhythm
Starts to boogie in your feet.

It jumps off the pavement,
There's a snare drum in your brain,
It pumps through your heart
Like a diesel train.

There's Harry on the corner,
Sings, 'How she goin' boy?'
To loose and easy Winston
With his brother Leroy.

Shout, 'Hello,' to Billy Brisket
With his tripe and cows heels,
Blood stained rabbits
And trays of live eels.

Maltese Tony
Smoking in the shade
Keeping one good eye
On the amusement arcade.
And everybody's talking;

Move along
Step this way
Here's a bargain
What you say?
Mind your backs
Here's your stop
More fares?
Room on top.

Neon lights and take aways
Gangs of boys and girls
Football crowds and market stalls
Taxi cabs and noise

From the city cafés
On the smokey breeze
Smells of Indian cooking
Greek and Cantonese

Well some people like suburban life
Some people like the sea
Other's like the countryside
But it's the city
Yes it's the city
It's the city life
For me.

Gareth Owen

The People Upstairs

The people upstairs all practise ballet.
Their living room is a bowling alley
Their bedroom is full of conducted tours.
Their radio is louder than yours,
They celebrate week-ends all the week.
When they take a shower, your ceilings leak.
They try to get their parties to mix
By supplying their guests with Pogo sticks,
And when their orgy at last abates,
They go to the bathroom on roller skates.
I might love the people upstairs wondrous
If instead of above us, they just lived under us.

Ogden Nash

P. C. Plod versus
the Dale St Dogstrangler

For several months
Liverpool was held in the grip of fear
by a dogstrangler most devilish,
who roamed the streets after dark
looking for strays. Finding one
he would tickle it seductively
about the body to gain its confidence,
then lead it down a deserted backstreet
where he would strangle the poor brute.
Hardly a night passed without somebody's
faithful fourlegged friend being dispatched
to that Golden Kennel in the sky.

The public were warned:
At the very first sign
of anything suspicious,
ring Canine-nine-nine.

Nine o'clock on the evening of January 11th
sees P. C. Plod on the corner
of Dale St and Sir Thomas St
disguised as a Welsh collie.
It is part of a daring plan to apprehend the strangler.
For though it is a wet and moonless night,
Plod is cheered in the knowledge
that the whole of the Liverpool City Constabulary
is on the beat that night disguised as dogs.

Not ten minutes earlier, a pekinese
(Policewoman Hodges)
had scampered past on her way to Clayton Square.

For Plod, the night passed uneventfully
and so in the morning he was horrified to learn
that no less than fourteen policemen and policewomen
had been tickled and strangled during the night.

The public were horrified
The Commissioner aghast
Something had to be done
And fast.

P. C. Plod (wise as a brace of owls)
met the challenge magnificently
and submitted an idea so startling in its vision
so audacious in its conception
that the Commissioner gasped
before ordering all dogs in the city
to be thereinafter disguised as fuzz.
The plan worked
and the dogstrangler was heard of no more.

Cops and mongrels
like P. C.s in a pod
To a grateful public
Plod was God.

So next time you're up in Liverpool
take a closer look
at that policeman on pointduty,
he might well be a copper spaniel.

Roger McGough

Pioneer

Who needs jungles for excitement
Climbing mountains fording streams
Risking life and limb in London's
Quite enough for me

Pebble dash to scrape your elbows
Paving slabs to graze your knees
Kerbs and gutters turn your ankles
Quite enough for me

Trucks that thunder down the street
The car that never seems to see
A cyclist or a zebra crossing's
Quite enough for me

And in the park there's stinging nettles
Clawing roses file-barked trees
Dogs and what they leave behind it's
Quite enough for me

And vicious beasts I've got as well
A cat that spits and brings in fleas
With spiders prowling round the bath that's
Quite enough for me

So keep your tigers sharks piranhas
I'll just stay in Palmers Green
Being bold in our back garden's
Quite enough for me

Mick Gowar

Birmingham

The children play over brick walls
and skip on concrete slabs
No trees to climb
No streams to dam
No daring hunt in a haunted wood.
Only a dodging dash from
verge to verge
along the motorway.

Laurence Smith

Where?

Where do all the buses go from the end of the street?
And where has that aeroplane come from, where?
What is it like at the end of the line?
How long would it take me to get there?

Is it the same there as here?
Are the schoolteachers kind,
Do policemen not mind
When you ask them to tell you the time?
And if you get lost do the folk lend a hand,
Or do they stare down
With a cold distant frown
And jeer, in a language you can't understand?

Where does the path end, going through the dark wood?
Where do the trains come from that pass in the night?
Where does the road end that starts in our street
If you turn to the left, or the right?
Is it weird there or wonderful; forlorn, busy or queer –
Or ordinary, just like it is here?

Brian Lee

Writing Poems

Michael Rosen

Jill Campbell

Roger Mc Gough

Charles Causley

Rose Flint

Vernon Scannell

Norman Nicholson

Gerda Mayer

Word

The word bites like a fish
Shall I throw it back free
Arrowing to that sea
Where thoughts lash tail and fin?
Or shall I pull it in
To rhyme upon a dish?

Stephen Spender

Shallow Poem

I've thought of a poem.
I carry it carefully,
nervously, in my head,
like a saucer of milk;
in case I should spill some lines
before I can put them down.

Gerda Mayer

Insouciance

In and out of the dreary trenches
Trudging cheerily under the stars
I make for myself little poems
Delicate as a flock of doves.

They fly away like white-winged doves.

Allen Wingate

Primer Lesson

Look out how you use proud words.
When you let proud words go, it is
   not easy to call them back.
They wear long boots, hard boots; they
   walk off proud; they can't hear you
   calling —
Look out how you use proud words.

Carl Sandburg

An Apology

Owing to an increase
in the cost of printing
this poem will be less
than the normal length.

In the face of continued
economic crises, strikes,
unemployment and V.A.T.
it offers no solutions.

Moreover, because of
a recent work-to-rule
imposed by the poet
it doesn't even rhyme.

Roger McGough

A Bottle of Ink

a black thread
reaching from here
to God knows where,
a thread to be broken
every black inch
of its blind way,
into the labyrinth.
Tonight I have written
letters that say

I love you and
These days my
poems die
under my hand . . .

Signing my name
I wonder what
sentences lie
coiled in that squat
bottle from which those came,
and why we pay
out lines like this
knowing there is
no going back.

Jon Stallworthy

Driving motor-way madly

Driving motor-way madly
Through the dictionary
ETCETERA
Striving like an angry bookworm
Starved of print
Is no way
To write a poem.

Let it drop
Like a sycamore seed
Designedly un-planned
To root and grow.
Or drop helpless, but complete
Like calf from cow
Licked, raspingly, into life.

Never write it
While old Super-Eg's awake.
Wait until that bore has nodded off.
Then let out wild and gentle Id
To graze and wander, velvet haltered,
with Ego by his side.

Then pour the poem
On the page
Like pancake batter
In the smoke-hot pan
To choose its own shape,
And grow there
If it can.

Jill Campbell

The Poem

It is only a little twig
With a green bud at the end;
But if you plant it,
And water it,
And set it where the sun will be above it,
It will grow into a tall bush
With many flowers,
And leaves which thrust hither and thither
Sparkling.
From its roots will come freshness,
And beneath it the grass-blades
Will bend and recover themselves,
And clash one upon another
In the blowing wind.

But if you take my twig
And throw it into a closet
With mousetraps and blunted tools,
It will shrivel and waste.
And, some day,
When you open the door,
You will think it an old twisted nail,
And sweep it into the dust bin
With other rubbish.

Amy Lowell

Poetic Retrospect

I tried to keep the summer in my head,
   Words, wishes, double weather,
But when I looked in the hiding-place
My heart had drowned that summer away
And nothing remained but the echoing bone
   And a cold wind blowing.

I tried to put the summer in a poem,
   Words, wishes, double weather,
But when I looked at the empty paper
My heart had wept that season away
And nothing remained but the echoing pen
   In a cold wind blowing.

The summer will not stay in mind or poem,
   Words, wishes, double weather,
And what I seek in the hidden places
Drowned in the charity of my heart
And nothing remains but bits of paper
   In a cold wind blowing.

T. H. Jones

In my craft or sullen art

In my craft or sullen art
Exercised in the still night
When only the moon rages
And the lovers lie abed
With all their griefs in their arms,
I labour by singing light
Not for ambition or bread
Or the strut and trade of charms
On the ivory stages
But for the common wages
Of their most secret heart.

Not for the proud man apart
From the raging moon I write
On these spindrift pages
Not for the towering dead
With their nightingales and psalms
But for the lovers, their arms
Round the griefs of the ages,
Who pay no praise or wages
Nor heed my craft or art.

Dylan Thomas

A poem is
something that someone is saying
no louder, Pip, than my 'goodnight' –
words with a tune, which outstaying
their speaker travel as far
as that amazing, vibrant light
from a long-extinguished star.

Jon Stallworthy

Poems on similar themes from *Poems* and *Poems 2*

Snapshots
Poems   pages 21, 51, 79
Poems 2   pages 29, 33, 37, 39, 51, 71, 109, 110

Shapes
Poems   pages 10, 11, 12, 13, 14, 44

Wordplay
Poems   pages 4, 5, 14, 15, 19, 20, 40, 42, 43, 44, 51, 66, 77
Poems 2   pages 8, 9, 10, 12, 113

Conversations
Poems   pages 16, 17, 47
Poems 2   page 94

Colours
Poems   page 78
Poems 2   page 74

Images
Poems   pages 8, 22, 23, 24, 36, 39, 88, 58
Poems 2   pages 17, 27, 32, 42, 44, 46, 53–58, 66, 67, 96, 98

Rhyme
Poems   pages 6, 19, 21, 29
Poems 2   pages 6, 7

Ballads
Poems   pages 60, 62, 80
Poems 2   pages 40, 115

Sleep
Poems   pages 34, 54

Space
Poems   page 56

Apples
Poems   page 86

Town Life
Poems 2   pages 59–65

Index

Acknowledgements

Moira Andrew: 'Tree'. First published in *Schools' Poetry Review*. Reprinted by permission of the author. **Patricia Beer:** 'January to December' and 'Noises from the School' from *Selected Poems*. Reprinted by permission of Hutchinson Publishing Group Ltd. **Anne Beresford:** 'The Romanies in Town' from *The Lair* (Rapp & Carroll Ltd.) Used by permission. **John Blackie:** 'Space Pilot'. Reprinted by permission of Basil Blackwell and the author. **Keith Bosley:** 'Snake glides' from *And I Dance*. Reprinted by permission of Angus & Robertson (UK) Ltd. **Jill Campbell:** 'Driving motorway madly' and 'Sunday smells of bacon, eggs' are reprinted by permission of the author. **Charles Causley:** 'Round the Town' from *Figgie Hobbin* (Macmillan). Reprinted by permission of David Higham Associates Ltd. **Leonard Clark:** 'Green Winter' from *The Singing Time*, © 1980 Leonard Clark. Reprinted by permission of Hodder & Stoughton Children's Books. 'Bronze and Silver' from *Good Company*. Reprinted by permission of Dobson Books Ltd. **David Cooper:** 'Apple' from *Ways of Talking*. Reprinted by permission of Ward Lock Educational Co., Ltd. **John Corben:** 'In the Stable: Christmas Haiku'. Used by permission. **John Cotton:** 'In the Kitchen'. Reprinted by permission of the author. **e.e. cummings:** 'one' from *Complete Poems 1913–1962*. Reprinted by permission of Granada Publishing Ltd. **Roald Dahl:** 'Giants', from the list of characters appearing in *The BFG*. Reprinted by permission of Jonathan Cape Ltd., on behalf of the author. **Walter de la Mare:** 'Which?', 'The Ghost' and 'Silver'. Reprinted by permission of The Literary Trustees of Walter de la Mare and The Society of Authors as their representative. **Lord Alfred Douglas:** 'The Shark'. Reprinted by permission of Edward Colman, Literary Executor for The Lord Alfred Douglas Literary Estate. **John Drinkwater:** 'Moonlit Apples' from *Collected Poems*. Reprinted by permission of Sidgwick & Jackson. **Gavin Ewart:** 'The Quarrel'. Reprinted by permission of the author. **U. A. Fanthorpe:** 'The Colourblind Birdwatcher' from *Standing To* (Harry Chambers/Peterloo Poets). Reprinted by permission of the author. **Rose Flint:** 'Snowbuck' is previously unpublished and is © 1985 Rose Flint; 'Applemoon' is from *Borderlines*. Both are reprinted by permission of the author. **Frank Flynn:** 'Yes', © Frank Flynn 1984 from *The Candy-Floss Tree* by Gerda Mayer, Frank Flynn and Norman Nicholson (1984). Reprinted by permission of Oxford University Press. **Robert Froman:** 'Development' from *Seeing Things*, © 1974 Robert Froman. Reprinted by permission of the author. **Robert Frost:** 'After Apple Picking' from *The Poetry of Robert Frost*, edited by Edward Connery Lathem. Reprinted by permission of Jonathan Cape Ltd., for the Estate of Robert Frost. **John Fuller:** 'The Cricket' and 'Ant', 'Rat', 'Tiger' and 'Whale' from 'A Bestiary', all in *Come Aboard and Sail Away* (Salamander Press). Reprinted by permission of the author. **Leon Garfield:** 'Colours' from *Apprentices*. Reprinted by permission of William Heinemann Limited. **Barbara Giles:** 'Timely', © Barbara Giles 1983, from *Upright Downfall* by Barbara Giles, Roy Fuller and Adrian Rumble (1983). Reprinted by permission of Oxford University Press. **Mick Gowar:** 'Pioneer' from *Swings and Roundabouts*, © Mick Gowar 1981, published by Collins. **Arthur Guiterman:** 'Habits of the Hippo' from *Active Anthologies* (Blond Educational). **John Heath-Stubbs:** 'The Tree-Creeper' from *Parliament of Birds* (Chatto & Windus). Reprinted by permission of David Higham Associates Ltd. **Patricia Hubbell:** 'Shadows' from *Catch Me A Wind* (Atheneum). **T. E. Hulme:** 'Autumn' and 'Above the Dock' from *The Life and Opinions of T. E. Hulme*, edited by A. R. Jones and published by Victor Gollancz Ltd. **Karen Jackson:** 'All for an ice-cream' from *Ways of Talking*. Reprinted by permission of Ward Lock Educational Co., Ltd. **Brian Jones:** 'Apple Song' from *Spitfire on the Northern Line*, originally published by Chatto & Windus, now handled by The Bodley Head. Used with permission. **T. Harri Jones:** 'Poetic Retrospect' from *Collected Poems*. Reprinted by permission of J. D. Lewis & Sons Ltd. **Brian Lee:** 'Where?' from *Late Home* (Kestrel Books 1976) pp. 42–43. Copyright © 1976 by Brian Lee. Reprinted by permission of Penguin Books Ltd. **Laurie Lee:** 'Apples' from *My Many Coated Man*. Reprinted by permission of André Deutsch Ltd. **Patricia Lloyd:** 'Colour Dream' from *Everyman Will Shout*, edited by Roger Mansfield and Isobel Armstrong (1964), © OYUP 1964. Reprinted by permission of Oxford University Press. **Amy Lowell:** 'Wind and Silver' and 'The Poem' from *The Complete Poetical Works of Amy Lowell*. Copyright © 1955 by Houghton Mifflin Company, Copyright © renewed 1983 by Houghton Mifflin Company, Brinton P. Roberts, Esquire, and G. d'Andelot Belin, Esquire. Reprinted by permission of Houghton Mifflin Company. **Roger McGough:** 'PC Plod Versus the Dale St. Dog Strangler' and 'Pantomime Poem' from *After the Merrymaking*; 'An Apology' from *Holiday on Death Row*; 'Rabbit in Mixer Survives' from *Waving at Trains*. All reprinted by permission of Jonathan Cape Ltd., for the author: 'Bully Night', 'The Writer of this poem', 'The Leader', 'Zebra Crossing', 'Eye Sore' and 'Snow and Ice Poems' are all from *Sky in the Pie* (Penguin Books); 'Gruesome' is included in *You Tell Me* (Penguin Books). All reprinted by permission of A. D. Peters & Co., Ltd. **Wes Magee:** 'Week of Winter Weather'. Reprinted by permission of the author. **John Masefield:** 'The Unending Sky'. Reprinted by permission of The Society of Authors the Literary representative of the Estate of John Masefield. **Gerda Mayer:** 'The Crunch'; 'Under a Tree' from 'Autumn in Regent's Park (3)', and 'Poplar', all © Gerda Mayer 1984, from *The Candy-Floss Tree* by Gerda Mayer, Frank Flynn and Norman Nicholson (1984). Reprinted by permission of Oxford University Press: 'Shallow Poem' from *The Knockabout Show* (Chatto 1978). Reprinted by permission of the author. This poem first appeared in *Ambit*. **Eve Merriam:** 'Mean Song' from *There Is No Rhyme for Silver*. Published by Atheneum. Copyright © 1962 by Eve Merriam. Used by permission of the author. All rights reserved. **Edwin Morgan:** 'Space Poem 3: Off Course', 'The First Men on Mercury' and 'Apple's Song' all from *Poems of Thirty Years* (Carcanet). Reprinted by permission of the author. **Christian Morgenstern:** 'The Names of the Months' from *Gallows Songs* trans. Max Knight (University of California Press, 1963). Used by permission. **Ogden Nash:** 'The

Squid' and 'Sweet Dreams' from *Parents Keep Out*. Reproduced by permission of Curtis Brown Ltd., London on behalf of the Estate of Ogden Nash: 'I'll Tak the High Road Commission' and 'The People Upstairs' from *I Wouldn't Have Missed It*. Reprinted by permission of André Deutsch. **Norman Nicholson:** 'Halley's Comet', 'In a Word', 'Road Up', 'Five-inch Tall' and 'Off to Outer Space Tomorrow Morning' from *The Candy-Floss Tree*: 'Wall' from *Sea to the West* (Faber). Reprinted by permission of David Higham Associates Ltd. **Leslie Norris:** 'The Ballad of Billy Rose' from *Finding Gold* is reprinted by permission of the author and Chatto & Windus Ltd. **Gareth Owen:** 'Ping-pong' and 'Boredom' from *Salford Road* (Kestrel Books 1979) pp. 51–52, 37–40. Copyright © 1971, 1974, 1976, 1979 by Gareth Owen. Reprinted by permission of Penguin Books Ltd: 'Out in the City' from *Song of the City* (Fontana Paperbacks). Reprinted by permission of the author. **James Reeves:** 'Grey' from *The Wandering Moon*. Reprinted by permission of William Heinemann Ltd. **Alastair Reid:** 'Squishy Words', © Alastair Reid. Used by permission of the author. **Michael Richards:** 'Monday', 'An Exultation of Larks', 'An ABC of Shropshire Field Names' and 'Proverbial Alphabet'. Used by permission. **Michael Rosen:** 'Down Behind the Dustbin' and 'You Tell Me' from Roger McGough and Michael Rosen: *You Tell Me* (Puffin Books 1981) pp. 41–42, 12. Michael Rosen poems © Michael Rosen, 1979. This collection copyright © Penguin Books Ltd., 1979. Reprinted by permission of Penguin Books Ltd.; 'I'm the Youngest In Our House' from *Wouldn't You Like to Know*; '54321' from *Mind Your Own Business*. Both reprinted by permission of André Deutsch. **Adrian Rumble:** 'Burning, Burning Moonward' and 'The Eagle Has Landed', both © Adrian Rumble 1983, from *Upright Downfall* by Barbara Giles, Roy Fuller and Adrian Rumble (1983). By permission of Oxford University Press. **Carl Sandburg:** 'What's the matter up there?' and 'Yarns' excerpted from *The People, Yes*. Copyright 1936 by Harcourt Brace Jovanovich, renewed 1964 by Carl Sandburg: 'Red and White' from *Harvest Poems 1910–1960*. Copyright © 1960 by Carl Sandburg: 'Star Silver' from *The Sandburg Range*. Copyright © 1957 by Carl Sandburg: 'Primer Lesson' from *Slabs of The Sunburnt West*. Copyright 1922 by Harcourt Brace Jovanovich, Inc; renewed 1950 by Carl Sandburg. All reprinted by permission of Harcourt Brace Jovanovich Inc. **Clive Sansom:** 'Willow' and 'Magic' from *An English Year* (Methuen). Reprinted permission of David Higham Associates Ltd. **Siegfried Sassoon:** 'Falling Asleep' from *Collected Poems*. Reprinted by permission of George Sassoon. **Vernon Scannell:** 'View from a High Chair' from *Apple Raid* (Chatto). Reprinted by permission of the author: 'Rhyme-Time', © Vernon Scannell 1982, from *Catch The Light* by Laurence Smith, Gregory Harrison and Vernon Scannell (1982). Reprinted by permission of Oxford University Press. **Elaine Slater:** 'No Buts' from *Ways of Talking*. Reprinted by permission of Ward Lock Educational Co., Ltd. **Laurence Smith:** 'Birmingham', © Laurence Smith 1982, from *Catch The Light* by Laurence Smith, Gregory Harrison and Vernon Scannell (1982). Reprinted by permission of Oxford University Press. **Stephen Spender:** 'Word' from *Collected Poems*. Reprinted by permission of Faber & Faber Ltd. **Jon Stallworthy:** 'A Bottle of Ink' from *Hand In Hand*. Reprinted by permission of Chatto & Windus Ltd., for the author: 'A Poem Is' is reprinted by permission of the author. **Gordon Symes:** 'Town and Country' from *Treble Poets 3* (Chatto & Windus, 1977). Used by permission of the author and publisher. **Dylan Thomas:** 'In my craft or sullen art' from *Collected Poems* (J. M. Dent). Reprinted by permission of David Higham Associates Ltd. **Judith Thurman:** 'Flashlight' from *Flashlight and Other Poems* (Kestrel Books 1977) pp. 8–9. Copyright © 1976 by Judith Thurman. Reprinted by permission of Penguin Books Ltd. **Kit Wright:** 'Cleaning Ladies' from *Hot Dog and Other Poems* (Kestrel Books 1981) p. 65. Text copyright © 1981 Kit Wright. Reprinted by permission of Penguin Books Ltd: 'Ghosts' from *Rabbiting On* (Fontana Paperbacks). Used by permission of the publisher. **Jane Yolen:** 'Caterpillar's Lullaby', 'Mother Worm's Hum', 'The Troll to her Child' and 'Mother Owl's Song' from *Dragon Night*. Reprinted by permission of Methuen Children's Books. Every effort has been made to trace and contact copyright holders. We apologize for any errors or omissions in the above list and would be grateful to be notified of any corrections that should be incorporated in any future editions of this volume.